100 Great Breads

100 Great Breads

Paul Hollywood

Photographs by Neil Barclay

BARNES
& NOBLE
BOOKS
NEW YORK

First published in Great Britain in 2004 by Cassell Illustrated,
a division of Octopus Publishing Group Limited,

This edition published by Barnes & Noble, Inc.,
by arrangement with Cassell Illustrated

2004 Barnes & Noble Books

M 10 9 8 7 6 5 4 3 2 1

ISBN 0-7607-5886-7

A CIP catalogue record for this book is available from the British Library.

Edited by Victoria Alers-Hankey and Barbara Dixon
Photographs by Neil Barclay
Styled by Fanny Ward
Design by DW Design
Jacket design by Jo Knowles

Printed in China

Acknowledgments

This book is dedicated to my wife, Alexandra, and my special boy, Joshua.

I would like to thank my mother, Gill, and father, John, for encouraging me into the baking trade in the first place and for washing endless mountains of chef's whites. I'd also like to thank my mother-in-law, Gloria, for helping me with some great recipe ideas.

Above all, a special thank you to my wife, Alexandra, for her support, love, and patience during my career and the writing of this book.

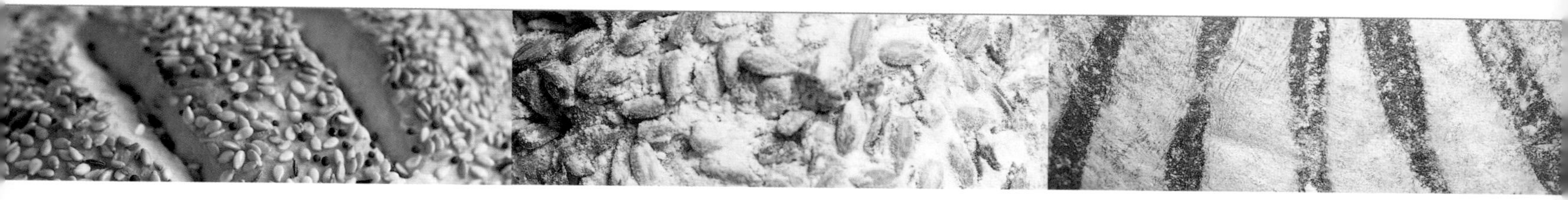

Contents

Introduction

Bread is the one natural food that has been with us for centuries, but in recent years it has been forgotten while we have indulged our passion for fast foods that are bursting with all kinds of additives.

I grew up in Liverpool, the oldest of three boys, and food to us was just a source of energy. It wasn't until I began to make bread in my father's bakery that I realized the variations and different types of bread were endless and that bread was not just the thick, white, sliced stuff to make bacon sandwiches with!

The aroma of freshly baked bread evokes feelings and memories in all of us—a snug kitchen in the winter after school and on the table a still warm loaf waiting to be smothered in butter and homemade strawberry jelly is one of my favorites, but who can resist ciabatta straight from the oven, stuffed with glossy black olives, garlic, and cilantro? Close your eyes and you're sitting on a vine-covered, sun-drenched terrace, sipping a glass of rich, red wine and surrounded by friends and family.

All the recipes in this book have special memories for me; some are from my childhood and some were discovered during my travels abroad. The textures and flavors all vary greatly, reflecting their origins, and I have added something of myself to all these recipes to make them unique and, I hope, satisfying to recreate.

Baking bread is a very sociable experience—you will find the whole family crowding into your kitchen, drawn by the irresistible fragrance of salmon brioche or a potato and rosemary focaccia. So pull up the chairs, break open a bottle, and enjoy the novel experience of eating a home-baked loaf of bread.

The History of Bread

I am a man who has bread in Heliopolis
My bread is in heaven with the Sun God,
My bread is on earth with Keb.

The bark of evening and of morning
Brings me the bread that is my meat
From the house of the Sun God.

(*Book Of The Dead,* Ancient Egypt)

From the depths of time, bread has been the one common factor that has linked the world's cultures together.

A recent excavation in Egypt, two miles south of the Sphinx, revealed an ancient bakery, complete with molds and working tools of the day. Meanwhile in London, builders working along the banks of the River Thames unearthed ancient loaves of bread dating back to Roman times.

The first breads were dense and unappealing—the grain was crushed and mixed with water to create a gruel, which was then left over a fire to cook hard. They were ideal for early man, being easy to carry on the hunt or into battle, and they would keep for days at a time, but they were not very appetizing.

It was the ancient Egyptians who took baking 10 steps farther. They discovered that the crushed grain and water mush, if left in a warm and moist atmosphere, would produce bubbles—the first sign of risen bread. This, mixed with fresh flour and then baked, would produce an aerated bread—and so the first yeast was created. Bread was incredibly important to the Egyptians. The poor lived almost exclusively on bread and it was used as a form of payment by the Pharaohs for work done on the pyramids and temples. Today's Egyptians still eat their meat or vegetables stuffed into loaves of bread, rather like a kabob.

The people of Israel were influenced by their contact with the Egyptians and began to produce a bread of their own. Theirs was a nomadic society, so until they settled, they baked their dough in the ashes of fires, producing a flat, cakelike bread. Later on, they began to build ovens and granaries, some of which, like those of the hill fortress of Masada, are still visible today.

The Greeks began by importing their corn from Egypt, but later began to cultivate their own crops. Grain equaled power in Ancient Greece, land owners were eligible for high offices when a certain standard of productivity was obtained, and in the 7th century BC the "Party of Bread"—the most prosperous farmers—ruled Athens.

The Roman Empire also imported their flour from overseas, from such places as Egypt and North Africa, and the Romans were responsible for the introduction of the water mill. These entrepreneurs also developed elegant tastes and many of their breads would still be acceptable today—sesame seed bread, almond bread, and milk bread, to name just three. After the Roman Empire collapsed, it appears that even as late as the 5th century, many Europeans were still making their bread at home.

The art of bread making progressed slowly during the Dark Ages and baking remained a family task in the villages and countryside for many hundreds of years. Eventually, communal ovens were introduced and, for a fee, bakers baked off the bread that was brought in. Some of these communal ovens are still currently in operation in France, where they consider the practice of bread making to be an art form.

Today, there are still people all over the world who bake their bread daily. The Bedouin in Petra, Jordan, bake on a bakestone, the modern version of which is a metal dome, lightly oiled and set over a flame. In some European countries, families still come together to bake bread and make it a social occasion, and some even have specially made ovens in their back gardens for just such an event.

Bread holds a social, religious, and gastronomic significance for all of us, but it is not just the act of breaking the bread that we should honor, but also the act of making or creating the bread.

Tools, Techniques, and Tips

Tools

There are only a few tools needed to make a good loaf:

1. Baking sheets and loaf pans
Any 1 lb/450 g traditional loaf pan is ideal for making breads. There are several varieties available, from Teflon to nonstick; some pans have straight sides, while others, such as farmhouse pans, tend to be more rounded.

Do remember to grease the pans—I use olive oil—before putting the dough in, as this will ensure that the bread doesn't stick.

Baking sheets are lined throughout—I line my sheets with silicone paper or parchment paper. Waxed paper tends to stick.

2. Ovens
I have made bread in or on every oven imaginable, from open-flame to fan-assisted to range cookers; all are great for baking bread. Every oven has a character, especially in professional bakeries, and hot spots are common. Get to know your oven, as it may have these elusive hotspots; use them when baking, and remember to turn your bread if the oven is a little hot at the back—the main reason for ovens being especially hot at the back is because over-impatient bakers look in the oven too often.

Most of the recipes in this book need oven temperatures between 400°–425°F/200°–220°C. This is more than enough heat to bake bread; most industrial bakeries bake at 475°F/240°C, the main reason being to keep moisture in the loaf. The longer a loaf takes to color or bake, the drier it will be.

3. A good serrated knife or a sharp blade
I have no preferences with the knives that I use—any will do, but just remember to keep them sharp: the cut on the bread is very important, not only for the look, but for the crumb texture.

Techniques

Yeast
There are two main types of yeast available in the supermarkets today—active dry and instant. Using active dry yeast means more work because you have to add water and sugar and let it froth. Instant yeast is more user-friendly because you throw it straight into the flour. However, be aware that this is a concentrated yeast and you will need less of it. All the recipes in this book use compressed fresh yeast, but I would suggest you use instant yeast if you can't obtain fresh—if you use instant or active dry, use 25 percent less than the recipe states. Compressed fresh yeast is available from most supermarkets nowadays—ask at the bakery department for a small amount and more often than not they will sell it to you. Failing that, ask at your local bakery.

Remember: all recipes use compressed fresh yeast, so if you are using instant or dry yeast, reduce the quantities a little.

Mixing the ingredients for the dough
When mixing the ingredients, avoid contact between the yeast and salt: salt kills yeast, which means the bread won't rise.

Kneading
Kneading is an important part of bread making. The way I knead is simple: start by making an indentation with the palms of your

hands into the middle of the dough—not too deep—then lift up the dough at the top and press it into the hole you have just made. Turn the dough and repeat, and keep repeating this process for the length of time stated in the recipe. The kneading times I give may fluctuate by 2 minutes each way as you get more proficient.

Adding flavorings to the dough

Always add any flavorings after the dough has been kneaded and rested for at least 1 hour, as this helps the dough to stabilize before it is pumped with any additions.

When adding ingredients such as onions and garlic—ingredients that are intrinsically acidic—do not add too much because this retards, or slows down, the rising of the dough.

Tips

- Use this book as a base, but try incorporating your own ingredients and experiment with flavors and textures.
- You do not always need to dissolve yeast in warm water; just throw it in.
- You do not always need to use warm water when making bread; the bread will rise anyway, even in the refrigerator. The slower the rising (proving) time, the more flavor the bread will have.
- The recipes in this book have measured water contents, but flours differ, so you may need a little extra water or a little less.
- When rolling out and kneading the dough, do not coat the counter in inches of flour. The dough will pick it up and tighten up too much.
- I do not normally cover the dough when it is resting; a little skinning on the top should be incorporated back into the dough.
- Always preheat your oven so that your bread has somewhere to go when it, and not you, is ready!
- None of the breads in this book require steam or pots of water in the oven. I like the crusty earthy look of home-baked bread—there's nothing better.
- I put most of my breads onto a cooling rack when they come out of the oven—this is to prevent the bread from sweating and going soft.
- Do not store baked bread in a refrigerator—it will go stale three times quicker than if left in a bread bin.

To help you with the skills needed to make bread, your first task is to make a cornsheaf loaf, which is a display bread and is pictured on page 9. If you can make a cornsheaf, you can make anything in this book. Before you begin, read the tips on the previous pages.

Cornsheaf Loaf

5½ cups white bread flour, plus extra for dusting
3 tbsp salt
2 cakes fresh yeast
¼ cup olive oil
1¾ cups water
1 egg, beaten, for eggwash

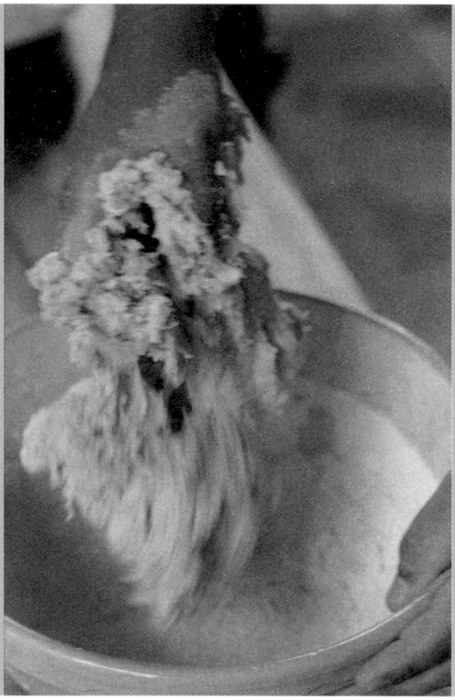

1. Put the flour in a bowl 12 inches/30.5 cm in diameter, then add the salt to the left and the yeast to the right. This is to avoid contact between the yeast and the salt (remember, salt kills yeast on contact, which means the bread won't rise). Although you do not need to avoid contact between the two when making a cornsheaf, it is a good practice to get into.

2. Add the olive oil and slowly start to add the water. (It's not necessary to use virgin olive oil since a lot of the flavor of the oil will be lost during baking.)

3. Begin squeezing the mixture together in your hands. Your aim is to pick up all the flour in the bowl with the water—you may need a little extra or a little less water. What you are looking for is a soft, pliable dough.

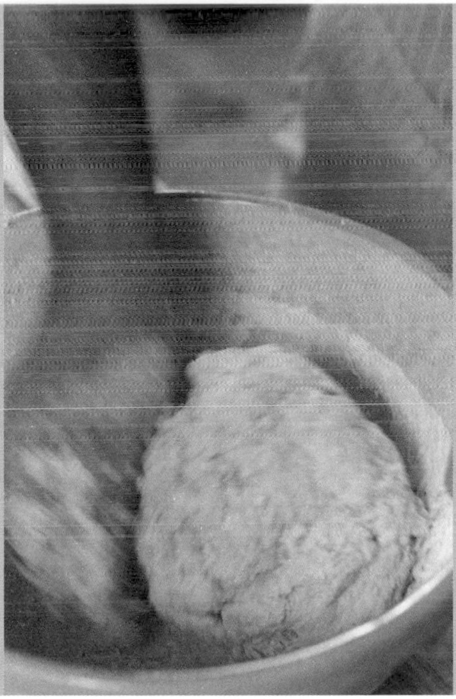

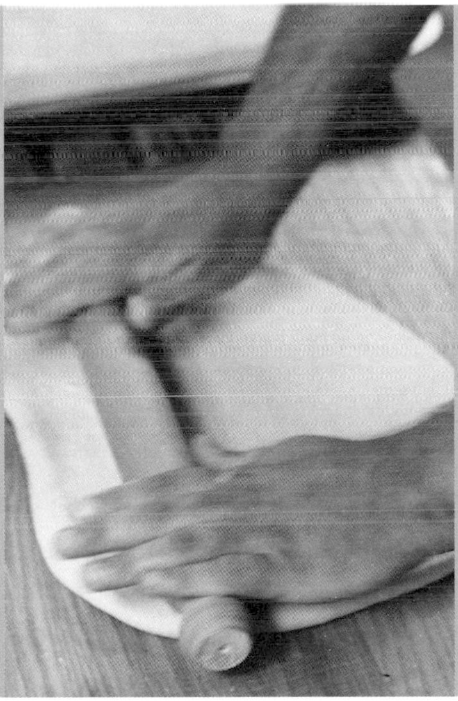

4. Now shape the dough roughly into a ball and tip it out onto a lightly floured counter. (I say lightly floured because most people make the fatal error of adding too much flour and tightening up the dough too much, and what started as a perfect dough ends up like a brick.)

5. Now you can begin kneading (see pages 12–13). Turn the dough 45° and make another indentation and fold in the top of the dough. Repeat this process for 10 minutes. With practice, you will eventually get quicker. Put the dough back in the bowl to rest for 1 hour. This is to let the dough relax and the yeast activate.

6. Rip off about a quarter of the dough and, using a rolling pin, roll it out to a rectangle, about 18 inches/45.5 cm long and ½ inch/1 cm thick—use a little flour to stop the rolling pin from attaching itself to the dough.

Cornsheaf Loaf (continued)

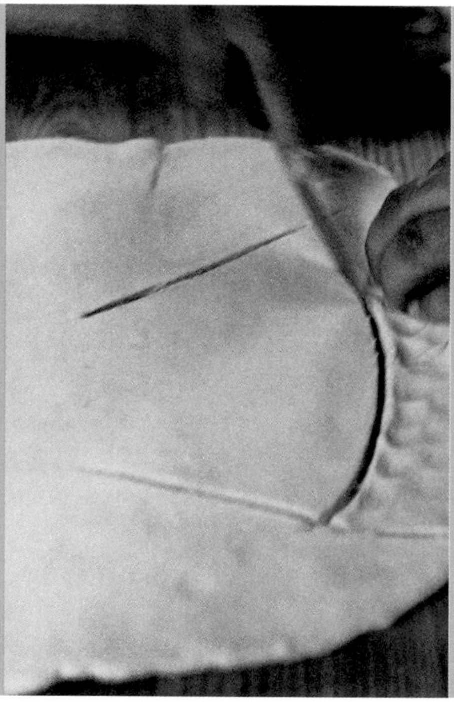

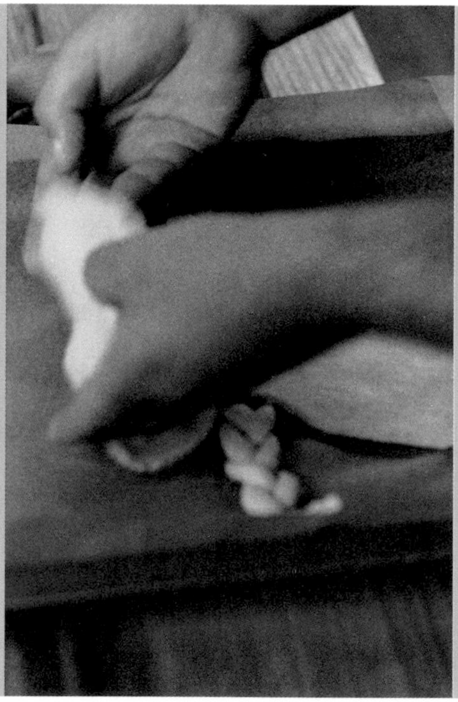

7. Using a knife, cut out a keyhole, or cornsheaf, shape from the dough, about 18 inches/45.5 cm long and 8 inches/ 20.5 cm across at the top, round end. Using the dough trimmings and extra dough, hand-roll out 20–30 pieces about 8 inches/20.5 cm long and as thin as you can get them. (When rolling dough, the trick is to use the full length of your hand, from your fingertips to your palms.)

8. To braid the dough, spread three strands in front of you and join them at the top. Cross the left one over the middle strand to the right and the right one over the middle strand to the left, then repeat until you have braided the whole length.

9. Line a baking sheet with baking parchment and put the keyhole dough on it. Carefully raise the round end of the cornsheaf dough and place the bread under it at the bottom, with the excess laid out on either side. Press firmly to flatten out the dough underneath.

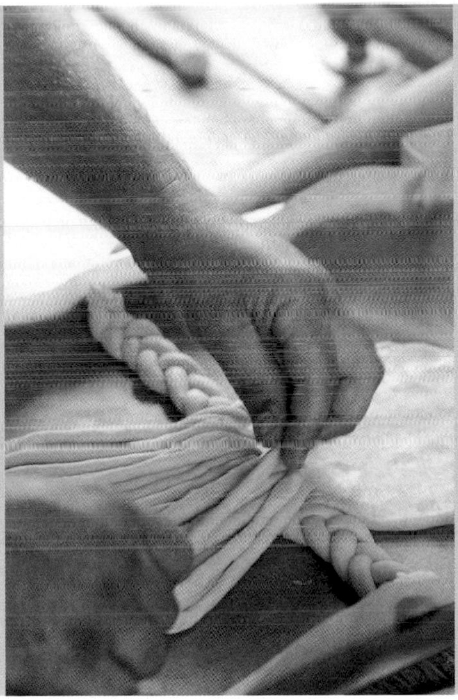

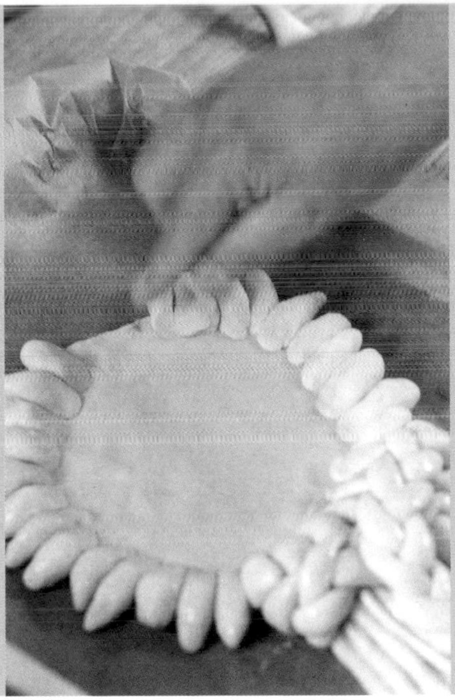

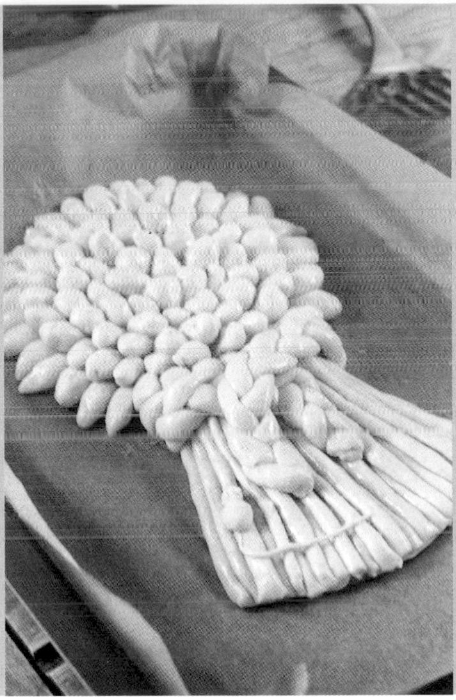

10. Brush the straight length with a little water, then begin adding the hand-rolled strands from the top of the straight length down to the bottom, to simulate the stems of the corn. When the base is covered, trim off any overhanging bits at the bottom, then reroll them and use to make a long-tailed mouse. Place the mouse toward the bottom of the stems of corn.

11. Next, rip off small pieces of dough and roll into balls, then slightly elongate them. Brush the round head of the dough with a little water. Place a row of balls to just overlap the top edge of the strips on the straight length, then add a row above. Fold in the two ends of the braid onto where the strips of dough meet the balls and press lightly to seal. Place balls all around the edge of the round head, then fill in the center with rows of balls just overlapping the previous row. Let the cornsheaf rest for 1 hour, to enable it to rise slightly.

12. Preheat the oven to 400°F/200°C. Brush the cornsheaf with the eggwash—this gives the baked bread a beautiful golden shine—and bake for 30 minutes. Lower the temperature to 300°F/150°C and bake for 30 minutes more. Cool on a wire rack.

Basic Breads

Remember to use a little olive oil to grease your loaf pans. Apply it with a cloth or a spray gun.

White Bread

scant 4 cups white bread flour, plus extra for dusting

1 tablespoon salt

¼ cup olive oil

1 package yeast

scant 1¼ cups water

Makes 1 x 1 lb/ 450 g loaf

Mix all the ingredients in a large bowl, taking care not to put the yeast on top of the salt. Knead well with your hands and knuckles, then let rise for 1 hour.

Oil a 1 lb/450 g loaf pan. Tip the dough out onto a lightly floured counter and mold into a sausage shape. Put back in the pan and let rise for 30 minutes–1 hour.

Preheat the oven to 450°F/230°C. Dust the top of the dough with flour, then put the pan in the oven and bake for 35 minutes.

Take out of the oven and turn the loaf out onto a wire rack to cool.

This bread, which dates back to medieval times, was known as one of the oven bottoms, as this was invariably where it was baked (as is the Farl on page 31). Baked to a deep color, it's a great British loaf—I remember watching my dad molding these when I was a kid.

Crusty Cob

scant 4 cups white bread flour, plus extra for dusting

1 tablespoon salt

1 oz/30 g yeast

generous ⅓ stick butter, softened

1¼ cups water

Makes 1 x 1 lb/ 450 g loaf

Put the flour, salt, yeast, and butter into a large bowl and mix together. Add nearly all the water and blend the ingredients together, then add the remaining water and mix in the bowl for 2 minutes.

Tip the dough out onto a lightly floured counter and knead well for 5 minutes, then place the dough back in the bowl and let rest for 2 hours.

Line a baking sheet. Shape the dough into a ball, then place on the baking sheet and let rise for 1 hour.

Preheat the oven to 425°F/220°C. Using a sharp knife, slash the dough across the top and dust with flour. Bake for 30 minutes, or until golden brown, then transfer to a wire rack to cool.

A very old British recipe, mainly baked during the eighteenth century, when white flour was prevalent. This sweet white loaf was favored by the "upper crust" of the country!

Batch Bread

scant 4 cups white bread flour, plus extra for dusting

1½ teaspoons salt

1 oz/30 g yeast

scant ⅔ stick butter, softened

scant ½ cup superfine sugar

1¼ cups water

Makes 1 loaf

Put all the ingredients into a large bowl and mix together. When all the flour has been picked up by the water, tip the dough out onto a lightly floured counter and knead for 5 minutes. If you find the dough sticks a lot to the counter, then dust lightly again with flour, but do not over-flour, as this will tighten the dough. Put the dough back in the bowl and let rest for 1 hour.

Line a baking sheet. Tip the dough out onto your floured counter and shape into a ball, then gently flatten it out with your hand until it is about 8 inches/ 20.5 cm in diameter. Dust the top with flour, then place on the baking sheet and let rise for 1–2 hours.

Preheat the oven to 400°F/200°C. Bake the loaf for 15–20 minutes, then transfer to a wire rack to cool.

The ubiquitous loaf the Brits have brought to the table. But I shouldn't mock. Made well, this is a beautiful bread—served as toast or as a simple sandwich, it's magic! The main recipe is for white bread, but try the whole-wheat version to help you understand the different textures.

White (or Whole-wheat) Pan Bread

scant 4 cups white bread flour, plus extra for dusting

1 tablespoon salt

1 oz/30 g yeast

½ stick butter, softened

scant 1¼ cups water

Makes 1 x 2 lb/ 900 g loaf or 2 x 1 lb/450 g loaves

Put the flour, salt, yeast, and butter into a bowl, then add the water, little by little, folding in with your hands until all the flour has been picked up. Tip out onto a lightly floured counter and knead for 5 minutes, or until you have a pliable, soft dough. Put the dough back in the bowl and let rest for 1 hour.

Oil the loaf pan or pans. Shape the dough to fit the pan(s), and let rise for 1 hour.

Preheat the oven to 450°F/230°C. Just before you bake the loaf, dust the top with flour and, using a knife, make slashes across the top. Bake for 30–35 minutes, then turn out of the pan(s) onto a wire rack to cool.

Variation: For Whole-wheat Pan Bread, use scant 2½ cups whole-wheat flour and ⅔ cup white flour instead of the scant 4 cups white flour, and use generous 1¼ cups of water. Proceed as above.

Basic Whole-wheat Bread

Whole-wheat flour does take more water than white flour. If you find that your particular flour needs more water than the quantity given, then by all means add more. Make the dough quite wet, because it does tighten up as the dough rests.

⅔ cup white bread flour, plus extra for dusting

scant 2½ cups whole-wheat flour

1½ teaspoons salt

1 oz/30 g yeast

½ stick butter, softened

1½ cups water

Makes 1 loaf

Put the flours, salt, yeast, and butter into a large bowl and mix together. Slowly add the water, mixing with your hand until all the flour has been incorporated from the sides of the bowl.

Tip the dough out onto a lightly floured counter and knead for 5–7 minutes. Put the dough back in the bowl and let rest for 1 hour.

Preheat the oven to 425°F/220°C. Line a baking sheet. Using a knife, cut a slash down the middle on top of the dough and dust the top with flour. Bake for 30 minutes, then transfer to a wire rack to cool.

Cottage Loaf

This bread is a very British shape. It originated some time around the 1500s and still exists in small village bakeries around the country.

2⅔ cups white bread flour, plus extra for dusting

1½ teaspoons salt

1 oz/30 g yeast

scamt ⅔ stick butter, softened

1 cup water

Makes 1 loaf

Put all the ingredients into a bowl and mix until you have a soft, pliable dough.

Tip the dough out onto a lightly floured counter and knead with your fingers for 5 minutes, then put back in the bowl and rest the dough for 1 hour.

Preheat the oven to 450°F/230°C. Tip the dough out onto your floured counter, then rip off a third of the dough and shape into a ball. Shape the remaining dough into a ball and place the smaller ball on top of the larger, then flatten slightly with your hand. Push your finger down through the center of the loaf from top to bottom until you can feel the counter. Dust the loaf with flour and, using a knife, make vertical slashes from the top of the loaf to the bottom (be careful not to cut yourself).

Put onto a lined baking sheet and bake for 30 minutes, or until golden brown. Transfer to a wire rack to cool.

When cooled, serve with chunks of cheese.

A friend started me on this. It was his birthday and he asked me if he could see his name in bread—better than in lights! These baked letters are not for eating, but for display only.

Named Bread

scant 4 cups white bread flour, plus extra for dusting

2½ tablespoons salt

2 cakes yeast

2 tablespoons olive oil

scant 1¼ cups water

1 egg, beaten, for eggwash

wood varnish, to glaze

Makes 400 small letters

Put all the ingredients into a bowl and mix well by rubbing in. Tip the dough out onto a lightly floured counter and knead for 6 minutes, then put the dough back in the bowl to rest for 1 hour.

Line several baking sheets. Divide the dough into however many letters you require, e.g. Paul needs 4, so cut 4 x 100 pieces of dough, and shape the dough into the required letters. Put the letters on the baking sheet so they are just touching, and let rest for 1 hour.

Preheat the oven to 425°F/220°C. Brush the letters liberally with eggwash, then put in the oven and bake for 30–40 minutes, or until they are a strong dark brown.

Transfer onto a wire rack to cool. The following day, coat the names with wood varnish to preserve them.

A very ancient bread. Milk has been used in bread for at least 1,500 years and it gives a characteristic flavor and a fairly tight texture.

Milk Loaf

scant 4 cups white bread flour, plus extra for dusting

1½ teaspoons salt

½ cup superfine sugar

⅔ stick butter, softened

1 oz/30 g yeast

1¼ cups milk

Makes 2 x 1 lb/450 g loaves

Put all the ingredients into a large bowl. Using a mixer, begin blending slowly, then speed up as you start to pick up all the flour. Alternatively, mix by hand.

Tip the dough out onto a lightly floured counter and knead for 5 minutes. Put the dough back in the bowl and let rise until doubled in size.

Tip the dough out onto your floured counter and divide into two pieces. Shape each piece roughly into a sausage shape and place crease-side down into two 1 lb/450 g loaf pans. Let rise for 1 hour.

Preheat the oven to 400°F/200°C. Bake the loaves for 25–30 minutes, or until golden brown, then turn out onto a wire rack to cool.

Dark Rye Bread *Illustrated*

This earthy, hearty, full-flavored loaf is from Eastern Europe. It will take up to 30 percent more water than most bread doughs. The recipe uses rye baskets—they can be bought in basketware stores or ordered through the Internet.

- **3 cups dark rye flour, plus extra for dusting**
- **scant 1 cup whole-wheat flour**
- **1½ teaspoons salt**
- **1 oz/30 g yeast**
- **4 tablespoons malt syrup**
- **2 tablespoons molasses**
- **scant 1¾ cups water**
- **2 teaspoons cumin seeds**

Makes 2 small loaves

Put 1½ cups of rye flour and scant ½ cup of whole-wheat flour into a bowl, then stir in the salt, yeast, malt syrup, and molasses and ⅔ cup of the water. Mix well for 5 minutes, then let stand in the bowl to rise for 5 hours.

Line a baking sheet. Add the remaining flours and water and the cumin seeds to the dough and mix well. Tip out onto a lightly floured counter, then divide the dough into two and shape each into an oblong sausage. Coat each sausage with rye flour, then place each in a rye basket and let rise for 2–3 hours.

Preheat the oven to 425°F/220°C. Tip each loaf out onto the baking sheet and bake in the oven for 35 minutes, then transfer to a wire rack to cool.

Irish Soda Bread

I've tweaked this recipe over the years and am finally proud of it. It's gorgeous served fresh from the oven with lots of butter.

- **scant 4 cups white bread flour, plus extra for dusting**
- **1 tablespoon baking powder**
- **1 teaspoon salt**
- **¾ stick butter, softened**
- **⅔ cups buttermilk**
- **⅓ cups milk**
- **2 medium eggs, beaten**

Makes 2 loaves

Put the flour, baking powder, and salt into a bowl and work in the butter. Stir in the remaining ingredients and mix well.

Line a baking sheet. Combine the mixture with your hands to make a dough, then divide the dough into two and shape into balls. Flatten the balls out and cut crosses in the top of each, then put on the baking sheet and let rest for 20 minutes.

Preheat the oven to 400°F/200°C. Dust the dough lightly with flour and bake in the oven for 30–40 minutes. Transfer to a wire rack to cool.

I first ate this bread, baked for me by monks, while staying in Roscrea Monastery in Ireland.

Whole-wheat Soda Bread *Illustrated*

1⅔ cups white bread flour, plus extra for dusting

1½ cups whole-wheat flour

1 tablespoon baking powder

scant ¼ cup superfine sugar

¾ stick butter, softened

scant 1¼ cups milk

2 tablespoons buttermilk

Makes 1 loaf

Preheat the oven to 400°F/200°C. Line a baking sheet. Put all the ingredients into a large bowl and work together to form a soft dough. Shape into a ball and flatten slightly and cut a cross into the top, then dust the top with a little flour.

Put onto the baking sheet and bake for 25 minutes, or until golden brown. Transfer to a wire rack to cool.

Variation: This bread can be made with 100 percent white flour—just replace the whole-wheat flour with 1⅔ cups of white flour. Proceed as above.

A nice twist on the traditional bread, and tastes fantastic!

Cheese and Onion Soda Bread

scant 4 cups white bread flour, plus extra for dusting

1½ teaspoons salt

1¼ cups buttermilk

2 tablespoons superfine sugar

¾ stick butter, softened

1 tablespoon baking powder

1 onion, peeled and finely chopped

¾ cup grated Cheddar cheese

Makes 2 loaves

Preheat the oven to 425°F/220°C. Line a baking sheet. Put all the ingredients except the onion and cheese in a food mixer and, using a paddle blade and medium speed, blend together for 2 minutes. Alternatively, put into a bowl and mix well by hand for 5 minutes. Add the onion and cheese and incorporate, either by hand or in the mixer (don't overmix), into the dough.

Divide the dough into two pieces and tip out onto a lightly floured counter. Shape each piece into a ball, then flatten each with your hand so they are approximately 2 inches/5 cm thick. Cut a deep cross into each, then dust with a little flour and put on the baking sheet.

Bake for 30 minutes, then serve warm.

Not that I drink a lot of beer (I prefer lager), but this bread is delicious! Serve with a good sharp Cheddar cheese.

Beer Bread

1½ cups whole-wheat flour

1⅔ cups white bread flour, plus extra for dusting

1 tablespoon salt

1 package yeast

¼ stick butter, softened

1¼ cups good beer

Makes 1 loaf

Put all the ingredients into a bowl and mix until all the flour has been picked up. Tip the dough out onto a lightly floured counter and knead for 5 minutes until the dough is smooth and creamy. Put the dough back into the bowl to rest for 1 hour.

Line a baking sheet. Tip the dough out onto your floured counter and shape into a ball, then flatten out with your hands and cut diagonal lines across the top. Put the dough on the baking sheet and let rise for 1 hour.

Preheat the oven to 400°F/200°C. Bake the loaf for 30 minutes until golden brown, then transfer to a wire rack to cool.

Another hearty loaf, with a little extra iron (i.e. Guinness). Eat yourself fit!

Guinness and Molasses Bread

generous 2 cups whole-wheat flour, plus extra for dusting

1 cup white bread flour, plus extra for dusting

1 tablespoon salt

1 oz/30 g yeast

2 tablespoons molasses

⅔ cup Guinness (stout)

½ cup water

Makes 1 loaf

Put all the ingredients into a large bowl and mix together for a few minutes. Tip the dough out onto a lightly floured counter and knead for 5 minutes, then put the dough back in the bowl and let rest for 1 hour.

Line a baking sheet. Tip the dough out onto your floured counter and shape into a ball, then flatten and roll up. Put the dough on the baking sheet and let rise for 1 hour.

Preheat the oven to 400°F/200°C. Cut several slashes across the bread and dust with whole-wheat flour. Bake for 30 minutes, then transfer to a wire rack to cool.

This bread is a favorite of mine, originally created for the Michelin-starred restaurant at the Dorchester Hotel. Serve as a sandwich, with crisp salad greens, roasted red and yellow bell peppers, and slivers of mustard-roasted beef. You need to start this the day before.

Stilton and Bacon Bread

scant 4 cups white bread flour, plus extra for dusting

generous 2 cups water

1 package yeast

1½ teaspoons salt

3 oz/75 g Stilton cheese, crumbled

4 oz/125 g bacon, chopped and fried

Makes 2 loaves

Put scant ¾ cup of the flour, ¼ cup of the water, and ½ oz/15 g of the yeast into a bowl and mix together by hand, then whisk with a hand whisk for about 5 minutes. Let rise in a warm place overnight.

The dough will now smell fermented, rather like beer. Add the remaining flour, water, and yeast and the salt, then knead well for 5 minutes. Let rest for 30 minutes.

Line a baking sheet. Tip the dough out onto a lightly floured counter and divide into two pieces. Add half the Stilton and half the bacon into each piece, then shape them into two circles and put on the baking sheet. Let prove for 1 hour.

Preheat the oven to 400°F/200°C. Dust the loaves with flour and bake for 30 minutes, then transfer to a wire rack to cool.

This multi-flavored and colored bread is ideal for indecisive families—there are rolls of four flavors in each loaf. It's great for dinner parties, too. The dough can be frozen when made, if not using immediately, and then defrosted overnight before baking.

Multi-flavored Bread

½ quantity Curried Naan Bread dough (see page 73)

½ quantity Date and Fig Bread dough (see page 104)

½ quantity Bell Pepper and Onion Flowerpot Bread dough (see page 88)

½ quantity Stilton and Walnut Whole-wheat Loaf dough (see page 103)

For the toppings

sesame seeds

poppy seeds

flour

grated cheese

Makes 3–4 loaves

Line 2 baking sheets. Make the doughs and divide them into 3½ oz/100 g pieces, then shape them into balls.

Place one ball of dough on the sheet and surround with 5 balls of different flavors. Make similar circles with the remaining balls, then let rise for 1 hour. The individual circles of dough will join up to form loaves.

Preheat the oven to 400°F/200°C. Bake for 25 minutes, then transfer to a wire rack to cool. Et voilà—multi flavors!

This bread is a very English loaf, traditionally baked on the bottom of the oven, hence its other name: oven bottoms!

Farl *Illustrated*

scant 4 cups white bread flour, plus extra for dusting

1 tablespoon salt

1 oz/30 g yeast

scant ⅔ cup stick butter, softened

1¼ cups water

Makes 1 large loaf

Put all the ingredients into a bowl and mix for 4 minutes. Tip out onto a lightly floured counter and knead for 5 minutes, or until the dough is smooth and pliable. Let stand in the bowl to rise for 1 hour.

Line a baking sheet. Tip the dough out onto your floured counter and shape into a ball, then flatten into a circle about 2 inches/5 cm thick. Put on the baking sheet and let rise for 1 hour.

Preheat the oven to 425°F/220°C. Cover the top of the dough with flour and, starting from the middle, make vertical slashes down the dough all the way round. Bake in the oven for 30 minutes, then transfer to a wire rack to cool.

These rolls are great for dinner parties—with three flavors to choose from, there's one to appeal to everyone.

Mixed Rolls

For the dough

scant 4 cups white bread flour, plus extra for dusting

1 tablespoon salt

scant ⅔ cup butter, softened

1 oz/30 g yeast

1¼ cups water

For the flavorings

¾ oz/20 g red or green bell peppers, deseeded and finely chopped, and ¾ oz/20 g onion, peeled and finely chopped

¾ oz/20 g Stilton, crumbled, and ¼ cup chopped walnuts

3 oz/75 g Brie, chopped, and a good handful freshly chopped basil

Makes 15–20 rolls

Put all the ingredients for the dough into a bowl and mix until all the flour has been picked up. Tip the dough out onto a lightly floured counter and knead for 5 minutes, then put the dough back in the bowl and let rest for 1 hour.

Line baking sheets and dust with a little flour. Divide the dough into three pieces. Incorporate the bell peppers and onions into one piece and divide into 3 oz/75 g balls. Place on a baking sheet and cut a cross on the top of each one.

Incorporate the Stilton and walnuts into the second piece of dough, then divide the dough into 3 oz pieces/75 g. Roll each into a sausage and tie in a knot, then place on a baking sheet.

Roll out the remaining piece of dough into a rectangle ½ inch/1 cm thick and scatter the top with the Brie and basil. Starting from the long side, then roll up the rectangle and press lightly on the edge to seal. Cut through the sausage every 2 inches/5 cm and place each piece, cut-side down, on a baking sheet. Let all the rolls rise for 1 hour.

Preheat the oven to 425°F/220°C. Bake the rolls for 20 minutes, then transfer to a wire rack to cool.

A traditional English afternoon tea favorite, served with clotted cream and strawberry jelly. I've worked in several five-star hotels and, as far as I'm concerned, afternoon tea is the best snack of the day—especially at Cliveden.

Scones *Illustrated*

scant 4 cups white bread flour, plus extra for dusting

2 medium eggs, beaten, plus 1 egg, beaten, for eggwash

scant ⅓ cup superfine sugar

1½ tablespoons baking powder

¾ stick butter, softened

1 cup milk

generous ½ cup golden raisins

Makes 15–18 biscuits

Preheat the oven to 425°F/220°C. Line a baking sheet.

Put all the ingredients except the eggwash and golden raisins into a food mixer and, using a paddle blade, mix for about 2 minutes on slow speed. If mixing by hand, this will take about 5 minutes.

Incorporate the golden raisins into the dough and tip out onto a lightly floured counter. Using a rolling pin, roll out the dough to about 2 inches/5 cm thick, then, using a round cutter, cut out the biscuits. (I normally use a 2–3 inch/5–7.5 cm cutter for the hotel-size biscuits.)

Put the biscuits on the baking sheet and brush with the eggwash. If you've the time, chill the eggwashed biscuits in the refrigerator for 30 minutes before baking to help with a straight rise.

Remove the biscuits from the refrigerator and brush the tops again with eggwash, being careful not to let it dribble down the sides, as this will hinder their rise in the oven. Bake for 15 minutes, then transfer to a wire rack to cool a little. Serve warm.

These are a particular favorite of a friend of mine, Chris Davies, who insisted I put the recipe in the book. If preferred, you may add ⅓ cup golden raisins to the dough when it has been formed.

Whole-wheat Scones

1⅔ cups white bread flour, plus extra for dusting

1½ cups whole-wheat flour

scant ⅓ cup superfine sugar

1½ tablespoons baking powder

¾ stick butter, softened

2 medium eggs, beaten, plus 1 egg, beaten, for eggwash

scant 1¼ cups milk

Makes 15–18 biscuits

Preheat the oven to 400°F/200°C. Line a baking sheet.

Put the flours, sugar, and baking powder into a large bowl and mix together.

Add the butter, eggs, and milk and, using your hands, mix together thoroughly for 6 minutes.

Turn the dough out onto a lightly floured counter and, using a rolling pin, flatten it to about 2 inches/5 cm thick. Using a round cutter (any size you like—I prefer to use 5–7.5 cm/2–3 inch cutters), cut out the biscuits.

Put the biscuits on the baking sheet and brush with the eggwash. If you've the time, chill the eggwashed biscuits in the refrigerator for 30 minutes before baking to help with a straight rise.

Remove the biscuits from the refrigerator and brush the tops again with eggwash, being careful not to let it dribble down the sides, as this will hinder their rise in the oven. Bake for 15–20 minutes until golden brown, then transfer to a wire rack to cool a little. Serve cool with strawberry jam.

Cheese and crackers is a marriage made in heaven. You can add 1 oz/30 g of golden raisins to the dough if you like.

Cheese Scones

scant 4 cups white bread flour, plus extra for dusting

2 tablespoons superfine sugar

1½ tablespoons baking powder

¾ stick butter, softened

2 eggs, beaten together, plus 1 egg, beaten, for eggwash

1 cup milk

1 cup grated Cheddar cheese

Makes 15 biscuits

Line a baking sheet. Put the flour, sugar, baking powder, butter, the 2 beaten eggs, and the milk into a bowl and bring together gently with your hands. When the dough has formed, add most of the cheese (reserving a little for sprinkling) and mix again for 5 minutes.

Tip the dough out onto a lightly floured counter and knead gently for 4 minutes until the dough is smooth. Roll out the dough to 1½ inches/ 4 cm thick and, using a cutter size of your choice, cut out the biscuits. Put the biscuits on the baking sheet, then brush the tops with the eggwash and put in the refrigerator for 30 minutes (this helps the biscuits to rise up straight).

Preheat the oven to 425°F/220°C. Remove the biscuits from the refrigerator and brush the tops again with eggwash, being careful not to let it dribble down the sides, as this will hinder their rise in the oven. Sprinkle a little cheese onto each biscuit and bake for 15 minutes, or until golden brown. Transfer to a wire rack to cool.

These crackers can be served as a snack or with cheese at the end of a meal. Any cheeses go well with them—they're great.

Cheese Crackers

2½ cups white bread flour, plus extra for dusting

1 teaspoon salt

1 stick butter, softened

scant ¼ cup water

2 medium eggs, beaten in separate bowls

For the flavorings

2 tablespoons poppy seeds

1½ oz/40 g Gruyère cheese

2 teaspoons caraway seeds

Makes 30–40 thin crackers

Put the flour, salt, butter, water, and 1 beaten egg into a bowl and mix well for 5 minutes.

Divide the dough into three pieces, and add the poppy seeds to one, the Gruyère to the second, and the caraway seeds to the third. Wrap each piece in plastic wrap and chill for 2 hours.

Preheat the oven to 220°C/425°F/mark 7. Line a baking sheet. Using a rolling pin, roll out each piece of dough on a lightly floured counter to about 3 mm/⅛ inch thick. Using a round cutter of your choice (I use one 7.5 cm/3 inches wide), cut out the dough. Place the disks on the baking sheet and brush with the remaining beaten egg.

Bake for 15 minutes until golden brown, then transfer onto a wire rack to cool. Serve warm or cold.

French Breads

The French are passionate about their bread—historically,, the shaving of bakers' heads for selling underweight bread was not uncommon. This loaf typifies French bread—a big, bold, hearty loaf full of flavor. Serve toasted or with cheese, it's a must try!

Pain de Campagne *Illustrated*

2⅔ cups white bread flour, plus extra for dusting

scant ⅔ cup rye flour

1 tablespoon salt

1 oz/30 g yeast

½ stick butter, softened

1 large bunch fresh oregano, destemmed and chopped

1¼ cups water

Makes 1 loaf

Put all the ingredients except the water into a bowl, then slowly add the water and mix in with your hands until all the flour on the sides of the bowl has been incorporated.

Tip the dough out onto a lightly floured counter and knead for 6 minutes. Put the dough back in the bowl and let stand for 2 hours.

Line a baking sheet. Tip the dough out onto your floured counter and shape into a ball, then slightly flatten with your hands and dust with flour. Using a knife, mark out a square shape on top of the dough, then put on the baking sheet and let rise for 1 hour.

Preheat the oven to 425°F/220°C. Bake for 30 minutes, or until golden brown, then transfer to a wire rack to cool.

The ubiquitous baguette, filled with cheese and ham and then toasted, is my lunch any day. Serve with a glass of chilled Chablis. Start this bread the day before.

Baguette

scant 4 cups white bread flour

1 package yeast

warm water to mix

1 tablespoon salt

½ stick butter, softened

Makes 1 loaf

Mix 1⅓ cups of the flour with all the yeast and enough warm water to make a thick batter, then let rise overnight.

Add the rest of the flour, the salt, and butter to the dough and slowly add enough water to make a soft, pliable dough. Rest the dough for 1 hour.

Line a baking sheet. Bang the air out of the dough and roll into a baguette shape. Put it on the baking sheet and let prove for 1 hour.

Preheat the oven to 425°F/220°C. Before the dough goes into the oven, using a sharp knife, make slashes along its length. Bake for 30 minutes, then transfer to a wire rack to cool.

This is a traditional French bread, flat and leaf-shaped, very much like the focaccia of Italy. It's eaten with cheese and salads. There are many flavors that go well in this style of bread—try bell peppers, ham, Cheddar cheese, or plain basil—c'est bon!

Onion and Bacon Fougasse

2⅔ cups white bread flour

1 oz/30 g yeast

generous ¾ cup water

1½ teaspoons salt

⅓ cup olive oil

1 onion, peeled, finely chopped, and fried until translucent

3 strips of Canadian bacon, finely chopped and fried

Makes 3 loaves

Line three baking sheets. Put 1⅓ cups of the flour with all the yeast and about ¾ cup of water into a bowl and beat together for about 3 minutes into a thick batter. Let rise and fall—this should take 3–4 hours.

Add the rest of the flour and water along with the salt, ¼ cup of the oil, the fried onions, and bacon and knead well for 5 minutes. Put back in the bowl and let rise for 1 hour.

Divide the dough into three pieces. Using a rolling pin, flatten each piece to about 2.5 cm/1 inch high, then shape each roughly into a circle. Using your knife, cut two diagonal slashes down the middle of each circle and three diagonal slashes on each side. Brush lightly with the remaining olive oil, then place on the baking sheets and let rise for 1 hour.

Preheat the oven to 450°F/230°C. Bake the bread for 15 minutes, or until golden brown, then transfer to a wire rack to cool.

I sold this by the truckful on Saturdays from our store in Canterbury.

Brie and Basil Bread

3⅓ cups whole-wheat flour, plus extra for dusting

scant ¼ cup olive oil

1 tablespoon salt

1 package yeast

water to mix

3½ oz/100 g Brie cheese, thinly sliced

a handful of freshly chopped basil leaves

Makes 1 loaf

Put the flour, olive oil, and salt into a large bowl and rub the mix together. Dilute the yeast in a little warm water and add to the bowl. Slowly add water, mixing with your hand as you do, until all the flour has been incorporated and your dough feels soft to the touch.

Tip the dough out onto a lightly floured counter and knead for 6 minutes, or until you have a pliable dough. Put back in the bowl and let rise for 2 hours.

Line a baking sheet. Tip the dough out onto your floured counter and, using your hands, shape into a mini baguette, then place on the baking sheet. Coat the top with whole-wheat flour and make several slashes in the dough lengthwise down the middle. Push the Brie and basil into the grooves, then rest the dough for 2 hours.

Preheat the oven to 400°F/200°C. Bake the bread for 20 minutes, or until golden brown, then transfer to a wire rack to cool.

A truly French bread. The immortal line uttered by Marie Antoinette, allegedly, "Let them eat cake," is more likely to have been "Let them eat brioche." You need to start this the day before.

Brioche Têtes

2½ cups white bread flour

scant ¼ cup superfine sugar

½ oz/15 g package yeast

1 teaspoon salt

⅓ cup milk

3 medium eggs, plus 1 egg, beaten, for eggwash

generous 1½ sticks butter, softened

8–10 paper muffin cases

Makes 8–10 brioche

Put the flour, sugar, yeast, salt, milk, and the 3 eggs in a food processor and process, using the blade, for about 5 minutes to a smooth dough. If mixing by hand, this will take 8 minutes.

Add the butter to the dough and mix for an additional 5 minutes in the mixer or 10 minutes by hand. Put the dough into a bowl, then cover and let stand in the refrigerator overnight.

The dough should now be stiff and easily shaped. Cut the dough into 3 oz/75 g pieces and cut one quarter off each piece. Using your hands, shape the quarters and the larger pieces into balls. Put each large piece of dough into a muffin case and push a smaller dough on top of each one. Let the brioche stand in a warm place to rise for 1 hour.

Preheat the oven to 400°F/200°C. Brush the brioche with the eggwash and bake for 15 minutes, or until golden brown. Transfer to a wire rack to cool.

Brioche was rumored to have been first made around the area where Brie is made, so this is a marriage made in heaven. You need to make the dough the day before.

Brie and Brioche Packages *Illustrated*

1 quantity Brioche dough (see page 43)

flour for dusting

9 oz/250 g Brie cheese

1 egg, beaten, for eggwash

Makes 1 brioche

Roll out the brioche dough on a lightly floured counter to about ¼ inch/5 mm thick. Place the cheese in the middle of the dough and fold the sides of the dough neatly onto the middle.

Turn the package over and brush the top with some of the eggwash, then place in the refrigerator for 1 hour.

Preheat the oven to 400°F/200°C. Line a baking sheet. Brush the package with eggwash again, then, using the back of a knife, score a criss-cross pattern over the package. Place on the baking sheet and bake for 15 minutes, or until golden brown. Serve warm.

During my time at the Dorchester Hotel in London, this brioche was a great favorite of the Sultan of Brunei. It's fabulous when toasted and served on a bed of arugula salad, with a lemon and dill vinaigrette. You need to make the dough the day before.

Salmon Brioche

scant 4 cups white bread flour, plus extra for dusting

1½ teaspoons salt

¼ cup superfine sugar

4 medium eggs

1 package yeast

scant ¼ cup milk

2¼ sticks butter, softened

5 oz/150 g smoked salmon, sliced

Makes 2 brioche

Put the flour into a bowl with the salt, sugar, eggs, and yeast and gently rub the mixture together. Add the milk, then use your hands to mix the ingredients together for 5 minutes. Let stand in a warm place to rest for 30 minutes.

Slowly add the butter to the dough, kneading for an additional 6 minutes, then stand in the refrigerator overnight. The dough will solidify.

Separate the dough into 16 pieces. Lightly cover your hands with flour and roll each piece into a small ball. Push your thumb halfway through the middle of each dough ball and place a slither of salmon inside. Reshape, using a little flour to stop the dough sticking to your hands, and repeat this process until you have 16 mini-brioche.

Grease and line two 1 lb/450 g loaf pans. Place eight of the balls closely together in each pan and let prove until they have reached three-quarters of the way up the pans—about 1 hour.

Preheat the oven to 400°F/200°C. Bake the brioche for 15 minutes, then turn out onto a wire rack and let cool slightly before serving.

Brioche is a delicate bread and, with the apricots inside, is a full breakfast in itself when toasted. You need to start this the day before.

Apricot Brioche

generous 2½ cups white bread flour

scant ¼ cup superfine sugar

½ oz/15 g package yeast

pinch of salt

⅓ cup milk

3 medium eggs

generous 1½ sticks butter, softened

1 cup soft dried apricots, diced

Makes 3 brioche

Put the flour, sugar, yeast, salt, milk, and eggs in a food processor and process, using the blade, for about 5 minutes to a smooth dough. If mixing by hand, this will take 8 minutes. Add the butter and mix for an additional 5 minutes in a mixer or 10 minutes by hand. Tip the dough out into a bowl, then cover and let stand in the refrigerator overnight.

Grease three 1 lb/450 g loaf pans. The dough should now be stiff and easily shaped. Divide the dough into 3 oz/75 g pieces and add 1 teaspoon of the apricots into the middle of each piece. Fold the dough over the filling and shape into little balls. Put the balls in the pans in rows of 2 balls, 1 ball, 2 balls, and so on until the pan is full. Each pan should hold no more than 10 pieces. Let the brioche stand for 1–2 hours to rise.

Preheat the oven to 400°F/200°C. Bake the brioche for 20 minutes, or until golden brown, then turn out and cool on a wire rack. Cut into slices, then toast and serve with lots of butter.

I've included croissants—although not essentially a bread—because they are risen with yeast and have become a symbol throughout the world for everything French. Every French pastry chef I've met has claimed he has the best recipe for croissants. I've tried and tested them all and come to the conclusion that mine are the best! Take a bite and see what you think. You need to start this the day before.

Croissant

1 package yeast

generous 4 cups white bread flour, plus extra for dusting

1½ teaspoons salt

generous ⅓ cup superfine sugar

water to mix

4½ sticks butter, chilled

1 egg, beaten, for eggwash

Makes about 40 croissants

Dilute the yeast with a little warm water and put with the flour, salt, and sugar into a large mixing bowl. Using a wooden spoon, slowly mix in a little water until the dough becomes pliable. Tip the dough out onto a lightly floured counter and knead well until it feels elastic. Put the dough back in the bowl and let stand in the refrigerator for 1 hour.

Turn out the chilled dough onto your floured counter and roll it into a rectangle 24 x 12 inches/60 x 30.5 cm. Flatten the chilled butter into a rectangle about ½ inch/1 cm thick and lay it over two-thirds of the dough. Bring the uncovered third of the dough into the center, then fold the covered top third down, so that your dough is now in three layers. Give the dough package a quarter turn so that the fold is on the right. Return the dough to the refrigerator to chill for 1 hour.

Scatter some more flour over the counter and roll out the dough to the same-size rectangle as before. Repeat the folding process, one side on top of the other, and turn the dough again, then place the dough back in the refrigerator for 1 hour. Repeat this whole process twice more, then let the dough rest, wrapped in plastic wrap, overnight.

Line a baking sheet. Using a rolling pin, flatten the dough to ⅛ inch/3 mm thick and cut into 8 x 8 inch/20.5 x 20.5 cm squares. Cut each square diagonally, making two triangles. Lay the triangles on a lightly floured counter with the narrow points away from you, then roll each piece up from the edge nearest you, toward the point, ending with the tip underneath. Bend the ends round to make the traditional croissant shape. Put the croissants on the baking sheet and let rise for 1½ hours.

Preheat the oven to 400°F/200°C. Brush the croissants lightly with the eggwash and bake for 10–15 minutes, or until golden brown, then transfer to a wire rack to cool.

On cold winter nights in the bakery, I used to wait patiently for these to come out of the oven, still oozing with cheese. They're great with coffee or as a light snack.

Cheese and Ham Croissant

1 quantity Croissant dough (see page 48)

1 egg, beaten, for eggwash

For the filling

7 oz/200 g honey-glazed ham

generous 1¾ cups grated Cheddar cheese

Makes 30–40 croissants

Make the croissant dough as on page 48 up to the point where it is ready to shape. (At this stage, you do not have to use all the dough; it can be frozen and will keep for 2–3 months. To defrost the dough, bring out of the freezer the night before and thaw overnight.)

Line several baking sheets. Using a rolling pin, roll the dough out to a rectangle, ⅛ inch/3 mm thick. Cut the rectangle into 4 inch/10 cm strips, then cut each strip diagonally into triangles. Once you have the triangles for the croissant, cut replica shapes from the ham and place on the dough and top with a little grated cheese. Lay the triangles with the narrow points away from you, then roll each triangle up toward the point, ending with the tip underneath. Bend the ends round to make the traditional croissant shape. Put the croissants on the baking sheets, then brush with eggwash and let rise for 2 hours.

Preheat the oven to 400°F/200°C. Bake the croissants for 20 minutes, or until golden brown, then transfer to a wire rack to cool.

If there is no other recipe in this book you try, do try this—I promise you, it's heaven. And if you've fallen out with your partner, make these and you'll kiss and make up in no time!

Chocolate Croissants

1 quantity of Croissant dough (see page 48)

3 Terry's Chocolate Oranges (if unavailable use a good quality orange-flavored chocolate)

1 egg, beaten, for eggwash

apricot jelly, warmed, to glaze

Makes 30–40

Make the croissant dough as on page 48 up to the point where it is ready to shape.

Line several baking sheets. Roll out the dough to ⅛ inch/3 mm thick and cut into 3 x 5 inch/7.5 x 12.5 cm rectangles. Put a piece of a Chocolate Orange at the short end of each rectangle and roll up into a package. Brush each one with eggwash, then place on the baking sheet and let rise for 2 hours.

Preheat the oven to 400°F/200°C. Bake the croissants for 20 minutes, or until golden brown, then remove from the oven and brush each one with the apricot jelly.

Italian Breads

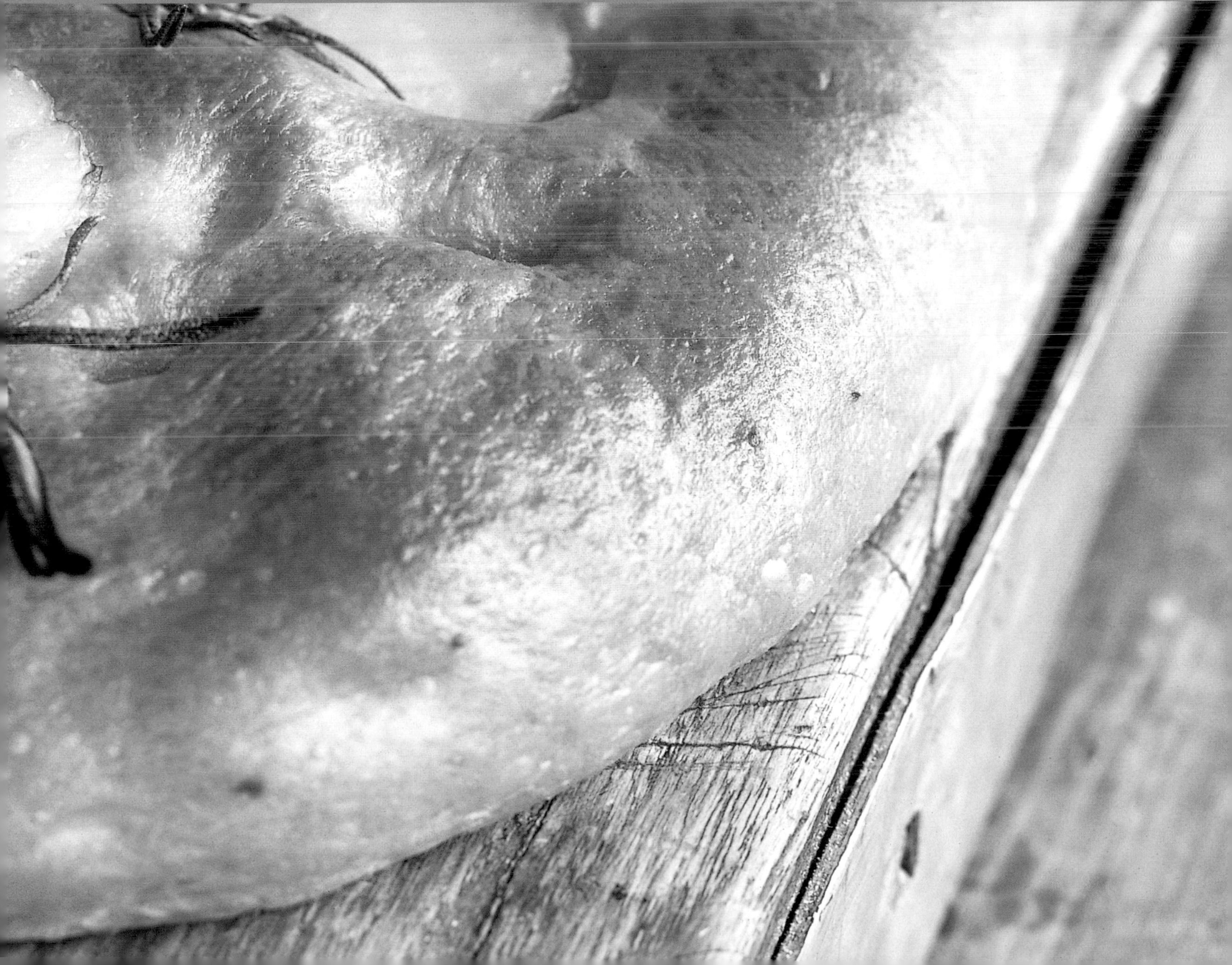

This recipe is perfect for making pizzas and garlic bread: simply flatten the dough out and use as a pizza base, or brush with garlic oil and you have instant garlic bread.

Ciabatta

scant 4 cups white bread flour, plus extra for dusting

generous 1½ cups water

1 oz/30 g yeast

1 tablespoon salt

2 tablespoons olive oil

Makes 4 loaves

Put 2 cups of the flour into a bowl with generous ¾ cup of water and the yeast. Using a hand whisk, whisk for 5 minutes, then let ferment for 4 hours.

Add the remaining flour and water, the salt, and olive oil. Whisk briskly for 5 minutes, then let rest in the bowl for 2 hours.

Tip the dough out onto a lightly floured counter and divide into two pieces. Stretch each piece of dough into a 8 inch/20.5 cm loaf, then let rest for 1 hour.

Line a baking sheet. Divide each piece of dough into two. Stretch each of the four loaves back to 8 inches/20.5 cm, then transfer to the baking sheet and let rest for 1 hour.

Preheat the oven to 400°F/200°C. Dust the loaves with flour and bake for 25–30 minutes, or until golden brown, then transfer to a wire rack to cool.

The idea for this pizza came from a Sicilian friend who had moved to Cyprus, where he had opened a pizzeria and built a beehive oven to bake the pizzas in. The secret of a good pizza is to use fresh ingredients and to keep the flavors simple—you want to be able to taste the ciabatta base and not have it overwhelmed by the toppings.

Ham and Cream Pizza

For the tomato sauce

2 tablespoons olive oil

1 small onion, peeled and finely chopped

1 garlic clove, peeled and chopped

1 tablespoon tomato paste

14 oz/400 g canned chopped tomatoes

2 tablespoons freshly chopped basil

2 bay leaves

1 teaspoon superfine sugar

salt and freshly ground black pepper

For the dough

1 quantity pizza (Ciabatta) dough (see page 54)

flour for dusting

2½ oz/60 g Gorgonzola blue cheese, crumbled

5 oz/150 g mozzarella cheese, crumbled

9 oz/250 g mature Cheddar cheese, crumbled

1 small carton heavy cream

8 thin slices of Smithfield ham

Makes 1 pizza

To make the sauce, heat the oil in a pan and sauté the onion until translucent, then add the garlic and cook gently for an additional 1 minute. Stir in the rest of the ingredients and season to taste. Bring the sauce to a boil, then let simmer for about 30 minutes. Before using, remove the bay leaves.

Meanwhile, preheat the oven to 450°F/230°C. Roll out the dough on a lightly floured counter to a 10 inch/25.5 cm diameter circle and place on a baking sheet. Bake for 5 minutes (this kills the yeast in the dough).

Lightly spread the tomato sauce onto your pizza base and sprinkle sparingly with the Gorgonzola, then cover with the mozzarella and Cheddar cheeses. Pour the heavy cream all over the pizza and bake for 20–25 minutes, or until golden brown.

Take the pizza out of the oven and place thin layers of ham on the top. Serve immediately.

Bruschetta is great party food and you can make it just a couple of hours before your guests arrive. It also makes a good snack.

Tomato Bruschetta

1 lb/450 g ripe tomatoes, peeled and cut into small pieces

3 tablespoons olive oil

10 basil leaves, torn in pieces

salt and freshly ground black pepper to taste

10–15 Ciabatta slices (see page 54)

2 garlic cloves, peeled and halved

Serves 4

Put the tomatoes in the oil with the basil leaves and season to taste, then let marinate.

Toast the Ciabatta, then rub each side with the garlic. Spoon some of the tomato mixture onto each slice and serve warm.

Olive Bruschetta

generous 1 cup black olives, pitted

juice of 1 lemon

1 tablespoon olive oil

salt and freshly ground black pepper to taste

10–15 ciabatta slices (see page 54)

2 garlic cloves, peeled and halved

Serves 4

Put the olives, lemon juice, and oil in a mixer and whiz for 2 minutes until you have a smooth paste. Season to taste.

Toast the ciabatta, then rub each side with the garlic. Cover each slice with the olive mixture and serve warm.

The aromas in your kitchen when making this are unbelievable. If you're trying to sell your house, make this an hour before the potential buyers view it. A sale is guaranteed.

Basil and Olive Focaccia

scant 4 cups white bread flour, plus extra for dusting

1 tablespoon salt

scant ½ cup olive oil

1 oz/30 g yeast

1¼ cups water

⅔ cup black olives, pitted but left whole

handful freshly chopped basil leaves

salt water made with 1½ tablespoons salt dissolved in scant ½ cup warm water

Makes 1 loaf

Put the flour, salt, half the olive oil, the yeast, and water into a large bowl and mix with your hand for 3 minutes, or until all the flour has been picked up.

Tip the dough out onto a lightly floured counter and knead well for 6 minutes. The dough should be quite sticky. Put the dough back in the bowl and let stand at room temperature for 2 hours.

Line a baking sheet. Mix generous ½ cup of the olives and all the basil into the dough, then flatten the dough out onto the baking sheet to about 1 inch/2.5 cm thick. Brush the top of the dough with a little olive oil and make indentations in the top with your fingers. Let rise for 1 hour.

Preheat the oven to 450°F/230°C. Brush the top of the dough with the salt water and drizzle with the remaining olive oil, then stud the remaining olives on top of the dough.

Bake for 25 minutes, or until golden brown, then transfer to a wire rack to cool a little. Serve warm with an olive salad.

This is based on a bread I made while working in Italy in 2002. You do not need the sun belting down—but it helps!

Focaccia Pugliese with Mozzarella

scant 4 cups white bread flour, plus extra for dusting

1 tablespoon salt

1 oz/30 g yeast

scant ½ cup olive oil

1¼ cups water

salt water made from 1½ tablespoons salt dissolved in scant ½ cup warm water

2 packages buffalo mozzarella, drained and crumbled

Makes 2 small or 1 large bread

Put the flour, salt, yeast, half the olive oil, and all the water into a bowl and mix together to make a pliable dough. Tip the dough out onto a lightly floured counter and knead for 5 minutes. Put the dough back in the bowl and let rest for 1 hour.

Line a baking sheet. Divide the dough into two pieces, or leave as 1 large bread. Stretch the dough out with your hands so it is about 2 inches/5 cm thick and oval in shape. Put it on the baking sheet and prick the top with a knife (this will restrict its growth). Brush the top with about 2 tablespoons of the salt water and the remaining olive oil. Cover the top of the bread with the mozzarella, then let the dough stand for 45 minutes to rise.

Preheat the oven to 425°F/220°C. Bake the bread for 30 minutes, then transfer to a wire rack to cool. Serve with an olive salad and a glass of good Tuscan wine like Montelpulciano.

Focaccia are both gorgeous to look at and to eat. They epitomize the Italian philosophy on bread—simple but effective flavorings. You will need to prepare the garlic oil the night before.

Focaccia Pugliese with Tomatoes and Garlic

4 garlic cloves, peeled and crushed

⅓ cup olive oil

scant 4 cups white bread flour, plus extra for dusting

1 tablespoon salt

1 package yeast

1¼ cups water

salt water made from 1½ tablespoons salt dissolved in scant ½ cupwarm water

6 plum tomatoes, thinly sliced

Makes 1 loaf

Add the garlic to the olive oil, then let infuse overnight, but for no longer than that.

Put the flour, salt, yeast, half the infused olive oil, and all the water into a large bowl and mix together for 4 minutes. Tip out onto a lightly floured counter and knead for 6 minutes, then put back in the bowl to rest for 1 hour.

Line a baking sheet. Tip the dough out onto your floured counter and roll out a rectangle about 1 inch/2.5 cm thick. Sprinkle with the salt water and the remaining olive oil, then, using a knife, prick the top of the dough all over. Place the tomatoes on top of the dough, then put on the baking sheet and let rise for 1 hour.

Preheat the oven to 425°F/220°C. Bake the bread for 25–30 minutes, or until golden brown. Eat warm.

I made this with a couple of Sicilian friends when I was in Italy, and was astounded by the flavors from the potatoes—they marry so well with the rosemary and bread.

Potato Focaccia Pugliese

scant 4 cups white bread flour, plus extra for dusting

1 tablespoon salt

1 package yeast

1¼ cups water

olive oil

8–10 new potatoes, scrubbed and thinly sliced

rock salt, to sprinkle

2 sprigs fresh rosemary, destemmed

Makes 1 loaf

Put the flour, salt, yeast, and water into a bowl and mix to form a dough. Let stand in the bowl for about 1 hour to double in size.

Line a baking sheet. Tip the dough out of the bowl onto the baking sheet and flatten with your hands, then brush with olive oil and, using your fingers, make indentations over the surface. Layer the potatoes over the top, then sprinkle with a little rock salt and stud with the rosemary sprigs. Let rise on the baking sheet for 1 hour.

Preheat the oven to 450°F/230°C. Bake the bread for 30 minutes. Remove from the oven and brush the loaf with more olive oil, then transfer to a wire rack and serve when cooled.

This focaccia perfectly complements tomato-based pasta dishes and thick winter soups. For extra richness, drizzle over a little olive oil and sprinkle with chopped garlic.

Mushroom, Onion, and Basil Focaccia

scant 4 cups white bread flour

1½ teaspoons salt

½ oz/15 g package yeast

¼ cup olive oil, plus extra for frying and drizzling

water to mix

2 cups chopped white mushrooms

3 onions, peeled and chopped

butter for frying

freshly chopped basil leaves

rock salt, for sprinkling

Makes 1 loaf

Put the flour, salt, and yeast into a bowl and mix thoroughly by hand. Add the olive oil, then slowly add sufficient water to make a dough. Mix until the dough comes away from the sides of the bowl. Tip the dough out onto a lightly floured counter and knead well for 5 minutes. When the dough is pliable, put back in the bowl, then cover and let rest for about 1 hour.

Meanwhile, cook the mushrooms and onions in a little butter and olive oil until browned. Set aside.

Add the mushrooms, onions, and a handful of chopped basil to the dough, pressing them into the mixture with your hands.

Grease a 12 inch/30.5 cm loaf pan. Transfer the dough to the pan and press out evenly to the edges. Let rest for 30 minutes.

Using your fingers, make indentations all over the dough, then brush lightly with olive oil and sprinkle with rock salt. Let prove for 1½ hours.

Preheat the oven to 400°F/200°C. Bake the bread for 20–30 minutes, or until golden brown. Eat warm.

You can try sunblushed tomatoes in this recipe—they work just as well. The aromas in your kitchen while you are making this bread will tempt not just you, but your neighbors, too.

Olive and Sun-dried Tomato Bread

scant 4 cups white bread flour, plus extra for dusting

1½ teaspoons salt

scant 3 tablespoons olive oil

1 package yeast

1¼ cups warm water

scant 1 cup black Greek olives, pitted

scant 2 cups sun-dried tomatoes, chopped

Makes 2 loaves

Put the flour in a large bowl and add the salt, olive oil, and yeast. Slowly add the warm water, folding it in with your hand until the dough becomes pliable.

Tip the dough out onto a lightly floured counter and knead for 5 minutes. Return the dough to the bowl, then cover and let rise for 1 hour in a warm place.

Line a baking sheet. Divide the dough into two and add half the olives and tomatoes to each piece and work in well. Mold into a round shape and press firmly down to flatten. Sprinkle flour over each dough and mark a cross in each. Put on the baking sheet and let prove for 1 hour in a warm place.

Preheat the oven to 425°F/220°C. Bake the breads for about 30 minutes, or until golden brown, then transfer to a wire rack to cool.

This is an Italian-inspired bread from Tuscany. Their tomatoes are so juicy and full of flavor that it was a natural thing to try them out in one of my breads.

Try drying the tomatoes yourself in an oven: cut them into slices and sprinkle with olive oil, then leave overnight in a low oven—225°F/110°C.

Tomato and Basil Bread

- scant 4 cups white bread flour, plus extra for dusting
- 1 tablespoon salt
- 1 oz/30 g yeast
- ¼ cup olive oil
- 1¼ cups water
- 3½ oz/100 g sunblushed tomatoes
- 2 packets fresh basil, coarsely chopped

Put the flour, salt, yeast, oil, and water into a bowl and mix gently by hand to bring them together. When all the flour has been incorporated, tip the dough out onto a lightly floured counter and knead for 5 minutes. When the dough is pliable, transfer it to a bowl, then cover and let rest for about 1 hour.

Line a baking sheet. Add the tomatoes and basil to the dough and work in well. Shape the dough into a long sausage and tie in a knot. Place on the tray and let rise for 1 hour.

Preheat the oven to 450°F/230°C. Bake the loaf for 30 minutes, or until golden brown, then transfer to a wire rack to cool.

You need to start this the day before.

Pane Tuscana

1 lb 2 oz/500 g Italian tipo 00 flour, plus extra for dusting

½ oz/15 g package yeast

1 cup water

¼ cup olive oil

Makes 1 loaf

Put half the flour, all the yeast, and ⅔ cup of the water into a bowl and mix until you have a thick batter consistency. Let rise for 9 hours or overnight.

Mix in the remaining flour and water and the olive oil and knead for 5 minutes. Let stand in the bowl for 1 hour to rise.

Line a baking sheet. Tip the dough out onto a lightly floured counter and shape into a ball. Rub flour all over the ball so it is covered, then make several slashes randomly all over the loaf. Let rise on the baking sheet for 1 hour.

Preheat the oven to 425°F/220°C. Bake the loaf for 30 minutes, then let cool slightly and serve warm.

I spent the summer of 2002 in and around Tuscany making bread with local bakers. This bread brings back good memories. The lack of salt in the recipe will be compensated for by the fermentation of the dough. You need to start this the day before.

Pane Tuscana with Dolcelatte Cheese

1 lb 2 oz/500 g Italian tipo 00 flour, plus extra for dusting

½ oz/15 g package yeast

1 cup water

¼ cup olive oil

5 oz/150 g Dolcelatte cheese

Makes 1 loaf

Mix half the flour with all the yeast and ⅔ cup of the water until you have a thick batter-like consistency. Let rise for 9 hours.

Line a baking sheet. Add the remaining flour and water and the olive oil to the dough and mix in well, then knead for 5 minutes. Slowly add the cheese—it will get very messy, but persevere, and add a little flour if it gets too wet. Roll up into a sausage and join the ends together. Dust with flour, then put on the baking sheet and let rise for 1 hour.

Preheat the oven to 425°F/220°C. Bake the bread for 30 minutes. Let cool a little and serve warm.

These make great snack food; my son, Joshua, loves them. They can be frozen in dough form and thawed in about 3 hours.

Grissini Sticks

1⅔ cups white bread flour, plus extra for dusting

pinch of salt

2 cakes yeast

1 large tablespoon olive oil

⅔ cup water

sesame or poppy seeds

Makes about 30 sticks

Put the flour, salt, yeast, and olive oil into a bowl and mix together. Gradually add the water (you probably won't need all of it) and mix until all the flour has been incorporated from the sides of the bowl. Tip the dough out onto a lightly floured counter and knead for 5 minutes. Return the dough to the bowl and let rest for 30 minutes.

Preheat the oven to 425°F/220°C. Line a baking sheet. Rip the dough into hand-size pieces and roll each out into thin strips about 10 inches/25.5 cm in length. Moisten your hands a little and roll each strip in sesame or poppy seeds, then place on the baking sheet. Bake for 20 minutes, or until golden brown.

This is a recipe that is used in several well-known hotels. The straws are very quick to make and when the pastry is baked it doubles in size and is a real mouthful.

Cheese Straws

1 package ready-made puff pastry

flour for dusting

1 egg, beaten

2 tablespoons paprika

7 oz/200 g Parmesan cheese, finely grated

Makes 30–40 sticks

Roll out the puff pastry on a lightly floured counter to about ½ inch/1 cm thick and brush with beaten egg. Sprinkle with paprika and coat generously with the Parmesan.

Fold one third in and then fold the remaining dough on top and rest the pastry in the refrigerator for 30 minutes. Repeat this twice more.

Preheat the oven to 400°F/200°C. Line a baking sheet. Roll out the dough to ½ inch/1 cm thick and cut into long strips. Twist each strip in opposite directions to create a spiral effect, then place on the baking sheet and bake for 15 minutes. Serve warm.

Traditional Breads

Authentic naan needs to be baked in a specially made brick oven, but I decided to shallow-fry the dough instead, which gives it this light and fluffy, golden finish. It's excellent as finger food, cut into thin slices and served with a chilled eggplant and sour cream dip.

Naan Bread

scant 4 cups white bread flour, plus extra for dusting

1½ teaspoons salt

½ oz/15 g yeast

water to mix

1 teaspoon cumin seeds

1 teaspoon caraway seeds

olive oil for frying

Makes 3 naan

Line a baking sheet. Put the flour, salt, and yeast into a bowl and add enough water to make a soft, but not sloppy dough. Add the seeds, then divide the dough into three pieces and put on the baking sheet. Let rest for 1 hour.

Turn the dough out onto a lightly floured counter and, using a rolling pin, flatten each piece into a circle, 10 inches/ 25.5 cm in diameter, and let rest for 5 minutes.

Heat a skillet to a medium heat and add a splash of olive oil. Shallow-fry each naan until browned on both sides, then set aside to cool slightly before serving.

I was asked by a chef to come up with a naan to go with his extensive buffet. I love curries so this was the obvious recipe.

Curried Naan Bread *Illustrated*

scant 4 cups white bread flour, plus extra for dusting

1½ teaspoons salt

1 tablespoon olive oil, plus extra for frying

2 tablespoons mild curry powder

½ oz/15 g package yeast

1¼ cups water

generous ½ cup golden raisins

3 tablespoons mango chutney

Makes 6 naan

Put the flour, salt, oil, curry powder, yeast, and water into a bowl and mix together for 2 minutes. Tip out onto a lightly floured counter and knead for 5 minutes, or until the dough is soft and pliable. Let rise for 30 minutes.

Line a baking sheet. Incorporate the golden raisins and chutney into the dough. Divide the dough into six pieces, then put on the baking sheet and let rest for 1 hour.

Turn the dough out onto a lightly floured counter and, using a rolling pin, flatten each piece into a circle, 25.5 cm/ 10 inches in diameter. Put back on the sheet and let rest for 5 minutes.

Heat a skillet to medium heat and add a splash of olive oil. Shallow-fry each dough until browned on both sides, then set aside to cool slightly before serving.

Paratha is a very moist, chewy bread—great for dunking in your curry. It can be fried in a skillet.

Paratha

scant 2½ cups whole-wheat flour, plus extra for dusting

3 tablespoons vegetable oil, plus extra for frying

salt

2½ cups water

For the filling

1 tablespoon vegetable oil

⅓ teaspoon cumin seeds

3 green chiles, deseeded and finely chopped

1 teaspoon ground coriander

1 oz/30 g golden raisins

Makes 4–6

Put the flour, oil, and salt into a large bowl and slowly mix in the water until a dough is formed. Knead until smooth, then cover the dough with a clean cloth and let stand for 20 minutes.

Meanwhile, make the filling. Heat the oil in a skillet and add the cumin seeds and chiles. Cook, stirring, for 1 minute, then add the coriander and golden raisins and mix well. Cook gently, stirring now and then, for 5 minutes, then put to one side.

Divide the dough into small balls and lightly coat each ball with flour. Roll each ball out on a lightly floured counter to form thin, flat breads, or parathas, about 2–4 inches/5–10 cm across.

Heat a grill pan until hot. Brush a paratha with a little oil and place on the grill pan. Add 2–3 tablespoons of the filling into the middle of the paratha and fold over to enclose. Once the paratha has cooked underneath, turn it over and cook the other side until golden brown.

Repeat the process with the remaining parathas. Serve warm.

This recipe haunted me for many a year while I was living in Cyprus—making 500 of these a day was not my idea of fun. But this is a great recipe, given to me by George Demitriades, ex-pastry chef at the Annabelle Hotel, Paphos.

The breads make a great pre-dinner nibble, served with drinks, or they can be eaten with cheese at the end of the meal.

Lavroche

1⅔ cups white bread flour, plus extra for dusting

generous ½ cup semolina

1½ teaspoons salt

1 tablespoon olive oil

scant ½ cup water

scant ¼ cup milk

1 egg, beaten, for eggwash

3½ oz/100 g sesame seeds

Fills 3 baking sheets

Put all the ingredients except the eggwash and sesame seeds into a bowl and mix well. Then, using your hands, knead for 5 minutes, or until you have a pliable dough.

Preheat the oven to 425°F/220°C. Line a baking sheet. Tip the dough out onto a lightly floured counter and, using a rolling pin, roll out until it is wafer thin—about ⅛ inch/ 2–3 mm thick. Use plenty of flour, but brush it off afterward.

Cut the dough into random shapes and place on three baking sheets, then brush each one with eggwash and coat the top with sesame seeds. Bake for 20–30 minutes, or until dark brown, then serve immediately.

This recipe comes from a tiny village called Kouklia, in the south of Cyprus. Breadmaking is a social occasion for Cypriots and I spent one marvellous afternoon with friends making bread for the whole village. Afterward we sat and ate the warm loaves with hummus, tzatziki, grilled meats, and salad—fantastic!

Cypriot Olive and Cilantro Bread

scant 4 cups white bread flour, plus extra for dusting

1½ teaspoons salt

2 tablespoons olive oil

1 oz/30 g yeast

1¼ cups warm water

scant 1 cup black Greek olives, pitted and chopped

3 oz/75 g onion, peeled and chopped

handful of cilantro leaves, chopped

Makes 2 loaves

Put the flour into a large bowl and add the salt and oil. Dilute the yeast in a little warm water and add to the mixture. Slowly add the warm water, folding it in with your hand until the dough becomes pliable.

Tip the dough out onto a lightly floured counter and knead for 5 minutes, then put the dough back in the bowl. Cover and let stand for 1 hour in a warm place.

Line a baking sheet. Divide the dough into two pieces and divide half the olives, onions, and cilantro between each piece. The dough will now be bulging. Mold each dough into a round shape and press firmly down. Sprinkle each lightly with flour and mark a cross in each one, then put them on the baking sheet and let stand in a warm place for 1 hour.

Preheat the oven to 425°F/220°C. Bake the loaves for 30 minutes, or until golden brown, then transfer to a wire rack to cool.

When I lived in Cyprus, I would visit the villages of my friends every Sunday and invariably make bread. This bread is very common in Cyprus and is best served with dips and a good olive salad. Mastika and mechlebe are spices and seeds used in many Greek/Cypriot dishes. They have a similar flavor to fennel or anise, which you can use to replace them. However, most good health food stores will stock them.

Koulouri–Cypriot Village Bread

- **pinch of mastika**
- **pinch of mechlebe**
- **scant 4 cups white bread flour, plus extra for dusting**
- **1½ teaspoons salt**
- **1 oz/30 g yeast**
- **¼ cup olive oil**
- **1¼ cups water**
- **3½ oz/100 g sesame seeds**
- **1 tablespoon black cumin seeds**
- **1 tablespoon caraway seeds**

Makes 1 loaf

Grind the mastika and mechlebe with a pestle and mortar to a smooth powder. Put the flour, salt, yeast, olive oil, and water in a large bowl and blend together. Add the mastika and mechlebe powder and knead for 5 minutes, then let the dough stand in the bowl to rest for 1 hour.

Tip the seeds into a large bowl and pour a little warm water on them just to dampen them. This will also balloon the sesame seeds and release their juice.

Line a baking sheet. Tip the dough out onto a lightly floured counter and shape into a ball. Drop the dough into the dampened seeds and turn until covered in the seeds, then place the dough on the baking sheet and let rise for 1 hour.

Preheat the oven to 425°F/220°C. Using a knife, make a cut around the middle of the ball and two on top. Bake in the oven for 30 minutes, or until golden brown, then transfer to a wire rack to cool.

This is a traditional Cypriot bread, and is eaten throughout the year in Cyprus.

Halloumi and Mint Bread

scant 4 cups white bread flour, plus extra for dusting

1 tablespoon salt

¼ cup olive oil

1 oz/30 g yeast

1¼ cups water

2 packets halloumi cheese, crumbled

scant ⅓ cup dried mint

Makes 1 loaf

Put the flour, salt, olive oil, and yeast into a bowl and slowly add enough water just to bring the ingredients together. Mix for 3 minutes, then tip out onto a lightly floured counter and knead for 5 minutes. (If you are using a food mixer, use the hook and mix for 5 minutes in total.) Put the dough back in the bowl and let rise for 1 hour.

Line a baking sheet. Add the cheese and dried mint to the dough and shape into a sausage. Taper the ends and place on the baking sheet to rest for 1 hour.

Preheat the oven to 425°F/220°C. Cut diagonal slashes across the top of the dough and dust with flour. Bake for 25–30 minutes, or until golden brown, then transfer to a wire rack to cool.

A traditional bread made in Cyprus around Green Monday, the day the fasting starts before Easter. The bread is usually eaten with fresh vegetables and fruit.

Try using ground fennel if mastika is difficult to get hold of, but any good health food store should stock it.

Laganes Bread

- 1 teaspoon mastika
- scant 4 cups white bread flour, plus extra for dusting
- 1 tablespoon salt
- 1 oz/30 g yeast
- ¼ cup olive oil
- 1¼ cups water
- 3½ oz/100 g sesame seeds
- 1 tablespoon caraway seeds
- 1½ tablespoons black cumin seeds

Makes 2 loaves

Grind the mastika with a mortar and pestle to a smooth powder. Put the flour, salt, yeast, olive oil, and water into a bowl and mix together for 3 minutes. Add the mastika powder to the dough, then tip the dough out onto a lightly floured counter. Using your fingers and the heel of your palm, knead for 5 minutes, then put the dough back in the bowl and let rise for 1 hour.

Meanwhile, put the sesame, caraway, and black cumin seeds into a bowl and pour over just enough warm water to cover. Let stand for 20 minutes—this balloons the seeds and releases their flavors.

Line a baking sheet. Tip the dough out onto your floured counter and divide into two pieces. Flatten each piece into an oval shape, 1–2 inches/2.5–5 cm thick, and turn them in the seed mixture until the dough is completely covered, top and bottom. Put onto the baking sheet and let rise for 1 hour.

Preheat the oven to 425°F/220°C. Using your finger, press holes over the top of the dough, then bake the loaves for 25 minutes, or until golden brown. Transfer to a wire rack to cool.

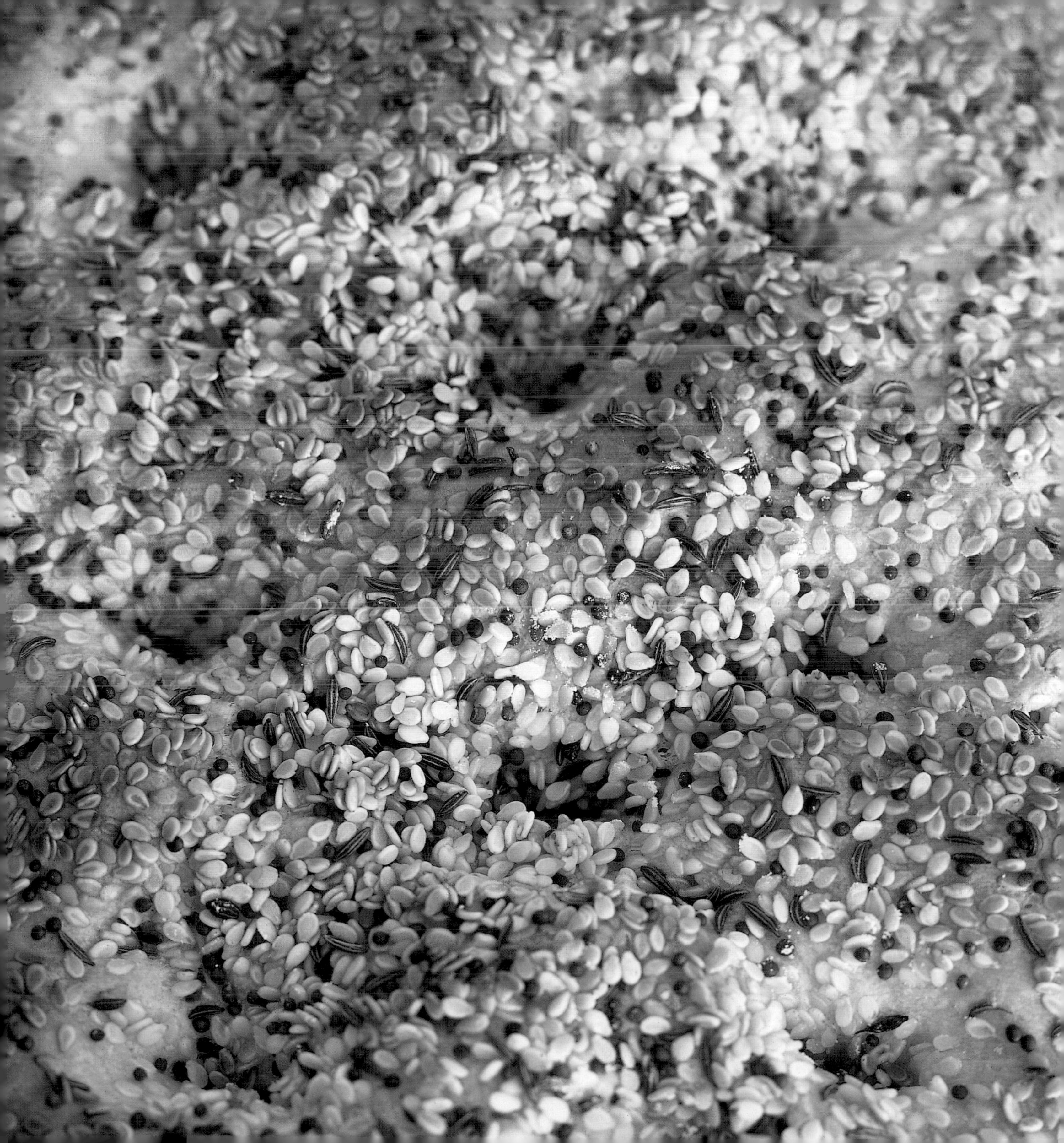

I have kept this bread as authentic as possible. You will find the mastika and mechlebe in any good health store, but you can use ground fennel as an alternative. I've made this bread several times on television and it remains a firm favorite.

Tsoureki—Cypriot Easter Bread

scant 4 cups white bread flour, plus extra for dusting

generous ½ stick butter, softened

generous ⅓ cup superfine sugar

pinch of cinnamon

pinch of mastika

pinch of mechlebe

handful of golden raisins

⅓ cup milk

zest of 1 orange

1 tablespoon salt

¾ cup yeast

⅓ cup warm water

3 eggs, hard-cooked in their shells with red food coloring

1 egg, beaten, for eggwash

Makes 1 loaf

Put the flour into a large bowl, then add all the other ingredients except the yeast, water, and eggs and mix together briefly. Dilute the yeast in a little warm water and add to the mixture. Slowly add the remaining warm water, mixing it in as you do, until you have a soft dough consistency.

Tip the dough out onto a lightly floured counter and knead until you have a pliable dough. Put the dough back in the bowl and let rest for 1 hour.

Line a baking sheet. Divide the dough into two and roll into strips. Braid the strips together, then put on the baking sheet and let rise in a warm place for 1 hour.

Preheat the oven to 400°F/200°C. Brush the top of the bread with eggwash and place the colored eggs along the top of the bread. Bake for 25 minutes, then transfer to a wire rack to cool.

A traditional bread made in Eastern Europe and shaped like the Russian Orthodox church. It makes a great afternoon treat.

Kulich

scant 4 cups white bread flour, plus extra for dusting

1½ teaspoons salt

generous ⅓ cup superfine sugar

¾ stick butter, softened

1 oz/30 g fresh yeast

vanilla extract

zest of 2 oranges

zest of 2 lemons

2 medium eggs

1¼ cups milk

generous ½ cup golden raisins

75 g/3 oz slivered almonds

lemon zest, confectioners' sugar, and water, for topping

Makes 2 loaves

Put the flour, salt, sugar, butter, yeast, a dash of vanilla extract, the orange and lemon zests, and eggs into a bowl and blend with a little milk just to bring the ingredients together. Slowly add the rest of the milk, mixing with your hands, until you have a soft dough.

Tip the dough out onto a lightly floured counter and knead for a few minutes. Put the dough back in the bowl and let rise for 1 hour.

Line two clean flowerpots or pans with silicone paper. Incorporate the golden raisins and almonds into the dough, then divide the dough into two and shape each piece so that it fits into the flowerpots or pans. Let rise for 1 hour.

Preheat the oven to 400°F/200°C. Bake the flowerpots or pans in the oven for 25–30 minutes, or until golden brown, then turn out onto a wire rack to cool.

When cooled, top with a water frosting made from lemon zest, confectioners' sugar, and water.

This recipe was given to me by Sylvia Woolf when I appeared on the *This Morning* show on British television. It has a great texture and flavor.

Pesach (Passover) Bread

9 oz/250 g medium matzo meal

1 teaspoon salt

1 teaspoon superfine sugar

1 cup water

½ cup oil

4 medium eggs

Makes 1 loaf

Put the matzo meal, salt, and sugar into a bowl and mix well.

Put the water and oil in a large pan and bring to a boil. Add the meal mixture and stir until the dough comes away from the sides.

Add the eggs, one at a time, and stir until the mixture is smooth and thick. Let cool.

Line a baking sheet. Flatten the dough out onto the tray and prick all over with a knife. Let it rest for 30 minutes.

Preheat the oven to 375°F/190°C. Bake the bread for about 30 minutes, or until browned.

A traditional Arabic bread that has been made for over 3,000 years. Originally it was made with a sour culture in place of yeast and baked on olive domes set over fires.

Pita Bread

scant 4 cups white bread flour, plus extra for dusting

1 tablespoon salt

¼ cup superfine sugar

¼ cup olive oil

1 oz/30 g yeast

1¼ cups water

Makes about 7

Put all the ingredients into a bowl and mix with your hands to bind together. When a dough has formed, tip out onto a lightly floured counter and knead for 5 minutes. Put back in the bowl and rest the dough for 1 hour.

Preheat the oven to 475°F/240°C and put a lined baking sheet inside to heat up. Tip the dough out onto the table and divide into 3½ oz/100 g pieces. Using a rolling pin, roll out the dough to about ½ inch/1 cm thickness. Let rest on the table for 5 minutes, then place on the hot baking sheet in the oven and bake for 5–10 minutes. The bread will balloon up, but when you bring them out of the oven they will collapse, forming the characteristic pockets of air.

The ancient Egyptians used to bake their bread in cone-shaped terracotta pots and this is the updated version, although the herbs and onions are authentic ingredients. This bread is particularly good for dinner parties—the little pots are very eye-catching and you could even try painting them for extra effect.

Bell Pepper and Onion Flowerpot Bread

1½ teaspoons salt

½ stick butter, softened

scant 4 cups white bread flour

1 package yeast

warm water to mix

2 large onions, peeled and finely chopped

olive oil for frying

scant ½ cup fresh basil leaves, coarsely chopped

3 red bell peppers, deseeded and finely chopped

Makes 3 loaves

You will need three flowerpots for this recipe, each 4 inches/10 cm in diameter and 25.5 cm/10 inches high.

Add the salt and butter to the flour and rub together. Dilute the yeast in a little water and add this to the flour, then mix in enough warm water to make the dough pliable. Knead the dough well for 5 minutes, or until elasticated. Place in a bowl, then cover and let stand in a warm place for 1 hour.

Cook the onions in a little olive oil until translucent, then set aside to cool. When cool, mix with the basil and bell peppers, then add to the dough and blend together. Divide the dough into three equal pieces and mold them into circles.

Line the insides and bottoms of the flowerpots with silicone paper. Place a ball of dough inside each pot and let prove for 1 hour.

Preheat the oven to 400°F/200°C. Bake the flowerpots for 30 minutes. Turn the breads out onto a wire rack to cool, then return them to the unlined flowerpots for display on your dining table.

Herb and Seed Breads

This is an aromatic bread, full of flavor. Basil is a favorite herb of mine, and is perfect mixed with the cilantro. This bread is great as the base for cheese on toast.

Herb Bread

scant 4 cups white bread flour, plus extra for dusting

1 tablespoon salt

1 oz/30 g yeast

⅓ cup olive oil

1¼ cups water

1 x ¾ oz/20 g package fresh basil

1 x ¾ oz/20 g package fresh cilantro

1 x ¾ oz/20 g package fresh dill

Makes 2 loaves

Put the flour, salt, yeast, olive oil, and water into a bowl and, using your hands, mix together for 3 minutes. When the dough has formed, tip out onto a lightly floured counter and, using your fingers and heel of your palm, knead for 6 minutes. Put the dough back in the bowl and let stand for 1 hour to rise.

Preheat the oven to 425°F/220°C. Line a baking sheet. Destem all the herbs, then rip them up coarsely and mix into the dough. Divide the dough into two pieces and shape each into a ball. Flatten slightly with your hands and cut two slashes across the top of each one. Place on the baking sheet and bake for 30 minutes. Transfer to a wire rack to cool.

You can also try making this recipe with Philadelphia cream cheese instead of the ricotta, for a creamy bread with tight airholes. Either way, it is unbeatable served toasted with cheese.

Ricotta and Chive Loaf

scant 4 cups white bread flour, plus extra for sprinkling

1½ teaspoons salt

1 oz/30 g yeast

⅓ cup olive oil

1¼ cups water

½ cup ricotta cheese

2 tablespoons snipped chives

Makes 1 loaf

Put the flour, salt, yeast, olive oil, water, and cheese into a large bowl and mix with your hands for 3 minutes. Tip out onto a lightly floured counter and knead for 2 minutes, then add the chives and knead for 3 minutes more. Put the dough back in the bowl and let rest for 1 hour.

Line a baking sheet. Tip the dough out onto a lightly floured counter and shape into a sausage shape, tapered at each end. Place the bread on the baking sheet and let rise for 1 hour.

Preheat the oven to 425°F/220°C. Bake the bread for 25 minutes, then transfer to a wire rack to cool.

This bread is definitely a meal on its own—serve it as a sandwich, sliced thinly, filled with roast garlic lamb and salad greens with a lemon dressing. It also makes a great accompaniment to a thick soup topped with cheese. You need to start this bread the day before.

Potato and Dill Bread

1 package yeast

water to mix

scant 4 cups white bread flour

1½ teaspoons salt

8 medium new potatoes, scrubbed

1 garlic clove, peeled and chopped

butter and olive oil, for frying

scant ½ cup fresh dill, destemmed and chopped

Makes 2 loaves

Dilute the yeast in a little warm water. Put the flour and salt into a bowl, and add the diluted yeast. Slowly add enough water to the flour until you have a malleable dough, then let rest overnight.

Boil the potatoes for 5 minutes and let cool, then cut into fourths. Cook the potatoes and garlic in a little butter and oil until golden brown, then let them cool.

Grease a baking sheet. Divide your dough into two pieces and flatten them into an oval shape. Place on the baking sheet and let rise for 1–2 hours.

Preheat the oven to 450°F/230°C. Cover the two pieces of dough equally with the potato mixture, pressing it in firmly. Sprinkle some dill over the top and bake in the oven for 25–30 minutes, or until golden brown. Transfer to a wire rack to cool.

A German-based rye bread, full of seeds. If this was a wine, it would be a full-bodied red.

Cereal Rye

- **generous 2 cups dark rye flour**
- **1 cup white bread flour, plus extra for dusting**
- **1½ teaspoons salt**
- **1 oz/30 g yeast**
- **⅓ cup malt syrup**
- **1¼ cups water**
- **2 teaspoons caraway seeds**
- **3 oz/75 g sunflower seeds**
- **3 oz/75 g sesame seeds**
- **1 tablespoon poppy seeds**

Makes 2 x 1 lb/ 450 g loaves

Put all the ingredients into a bowl and mix well. Knead gently for 5 minutes to bring together, then tip out onto a lightly floured counter and knead with your fingers and palms for 6 minutes. Put the dough back in the bowl and let rest for 2 hours.

Grease two 1 lb/450 g loaf pans. Divide the dough into two pieces and form each into a sausage shape. Put into the pans and let rise for 1 hour.

Preheat the oven to 425°F/220°C. Bake the loaves for 30 minutes, then turn out onto a wire rack to cool.

These breads have been spotted in bakeries around the Middle East, Greece, and in the tombs of the Pharoahs.
The rings can be cut open and filled with cheese and onion, to make a great snack.

Sesame Rings

scant 4 cups white bread flour, plus extra for dusting

1½ teaspoons salt

1 oz/30 g yeast

2 tablespoons olive oil

1¼ cups water

sesame seeds, to coat

Makes 10–15

Put all the ingredients except the sesame seeds into a bowl and roughly mix together. When the dough has formed, tip it onto a lightly floured counter and knead for 5 minutes. Put the dough back into the bowl and let double in size.

Line two baking sheets. Divide the dough into 3 oz/75 g pieces and roll them out to about 4 inch/10 cm-long sausage shapes, then join the ends to form a ring. When all the rings have been made, roll them in the sesame seeds and place them on the baking sheets, then let rise for 1 hour.

Preheat the oven to 425°F/220°C. Bake the rings for 25 minutes, or until golden brown, then transfer to a wire rack to cool.

Sunflower Seed Bread *Illustrated*

I was asked to make a bread for Spyros, a friend in Cyprus; he loved sunflower seeds, so I came up with this. I hope you like it. It will last longer if the butter is omitted, but it gives it a richer flavor.

1½ cups whole-wheat flour

1⅔ cups white bread flour, plus extra for dusting

1 tablespoon salt

1 oz/30 g yeast

½ stick butter (optional)

1¼ cups water

5 oz/150 g sunflower seeds

Makes 1 loaf

Put the flours, salt, yeast, butter (if using), and water into a large bowl and mix to a soft pliable dough (add a little extra water if necessary). Tip out onto a lightly floured counter and knead for 5–6 minutes until you have a very smooth dough, then put the dough back in the bowl and let rest for 1 hour.

Line a baking sheet. Incorporate the sunflower seeds into the dough, then shape the dough into a ball and flatten with your hands. Using a knife, make vertical slashes around the sides of the dough, from top to bottom, then roll the dough in any remaining seeds. Put onto the baking sheet and let rise in a warm place for 1 hour.

Preheat the oven to 425°F/220°C. Bake the loaf for 30 minutes, or until golden brown, then transfer to a wire rack to cool.

Rye with Caraway

This loaf you love or you hate, mainly because of the caraway seeds. You need to start this the night before.

2 cups rye flour, plus extra for dusting

1⅓ cups white bread flour, plus extra for dusting

1 oz/30 g yeast

1¼ cups water

1½ teaspoons salt

generous ½ stick butter, softened

2½ oz/60 g caraway seeds

Makes 1 loaf

Put half the rye flour, half the white flour, and all the yeast into a large bowl, then add about ¾ cup of water and mix well until you have a thick paste. Let this dough stand in the bowl overnight for 10–12 hours.

Add the rest of the flours, the salt, butter, caraway seeds, and remaining water and mix well in the bowl for 3 minutes. Tip out onto a lightly floured counter and knead well for 3 minutes, then put the dough back in the bowl and let rise for 1 hour.

Line a baking sheet. Tip the dough out onto your floured counter and roll into a ball. Then, using a rolling pin, flatten it slightly into a disc. Cover the top with rye flour, then put the dough on the baking sheet and let rise for 2 hours.

Preheat the oven to 425°F/220°C. Bake the loaf for 30 minutes, then serve warm with smoked salmon.

Fruit and Nut Breads

This bread was one of the first breads I made when I worked at the Chester Grosvenor Hotel. It was produced for the restaurant and went well with the cheeseboard. It's a real old favorite.

You can also make this bread with 100 percent white flour. This will give a slightly different texture.

Stilton and Walnut Whole-wheat Loaf

⅔ cup white bread flour, plus extra for dusting

scant 2½ cups whole-wheat flour

1 tablespoon salt

1 oz/30 g yeast

½ stick butter, softened

1¼ cups water

3½ oz/100 g Stilton cheese, crumbled

¾ cup chopped walnuts

Makes 1 loaf

Put the flours, salt, yeast, and butter into a bowl. Add the water, a little at a time, and gradually incorporate all the flour from the sides of the bowl.

Turn the dough out onto a lightly floured counter and knead for 5 minutes, or until the dough is smooth and pliable. Put back in the bowl and let rise for 1 hour.

Line a baking sheet. Add the Stilton and walnuts to the dough and mix well together. Divide the dough into three pieces and roll each one into a long sausage. Braid the dough—place the three strips side by side and join them at the top, then bring the right strip over the middle strip, then the left strip over, and continue until the braid is complete. Put on the tray and let rise for 1 hour.

Preheat the oven to 450°F/230°C. Bake the loaf for 30 minutes, then transfer to a wire rack to cool.

Made on Good Friday, this bread is eaten throughout the Easter weekend, so you can throw the chocolates away.

Fruit Bread

- **scant 4 cups white bread flour, plus extra for dusting**
- **1 tablespoon salt**
- **1 oz/30 g yeast**
- **generous ⅓ cup superfine sugar**
- **¾ stick butter, softened**
- **3 medium eggs, beaten**
- **1¼ cups milk and water mixed**
- **1 tablespoon ground cinnamon**
- **2 oz/50 g mandarin orange segments**
- **½ cup golden raisins**
- **generous ⅓ cup candied peel**
- **zest of 3 lemons**
- **zest of 3 oranges**

Makes 2 loaves

Put the flour, salt, yeast, sugar, butter, and eggs into a large bowl. Gradually add the milk and water mixture and bind the ingredients together for 3 minutes. Tip the dough out onto a lightly floured counter and knead for 5 minutes, then put the dough back in the bowl and let stand for 1½ hours to rise.

Line a baking sheet. Incorporate the cinnamon, mandarin oranges, golden raisins, candied peel, and zests into the dough, then divide the dough into two pieces and shape each into a ball. Flatten the balls to about 3 inches/7.5 cm thick, then, using a knife, score each piece into eight equal segments. Place the dough on the baking sheet and let rise for 1 hour.

Preheat the oven to 425°F/220°C. Bake the breads for 20 minutes, or until golden brown, then transfer to a wire rack to cool.

This is a moist, chewy bread packed with goodness. For me it's a breakfast bread, but it would be equally at home on a cheeseboard.

Date and Fig Bread *Illustrated*

- **scant 2½ cups whole-wheat flour**
- **⅔ cup white bread flour, plus extra for dusting**
- **1 tablespoon salt**
- **1 oz/30 g yeast**
- **½ stick butter, softened**
- **1 tablespoon molasses**
- **1¼ cups water**
- **½ cup dried figs, chopped**
- **½ cup dates, chopped**

Makes 2 small loaves

Put the flours, salt, yeast, butter, molasses, and water into a bowl and mix for 5 minutes. Tip out onto a lightly floured counter and knead for 5 minutes, then put the dough back in the bowl and let stand for 1 hour to rise.

Line a baking sheet. Incorporate the figs and dates into the dough, then divide it into two pieces. Shape the pieces into balls, then place on the baking sheet and let rise for 1 hour.

Preheat the oven to 425°F/220°C. Dust the loaves with flour and, using a knife, make three equidistant horizontal cuts all around each ball. Bake for 30 minutes, then transfer to a wire rack to cool.

This bread was inspired by a friend of mine, Chris Davies, an avid cook who wanted an unusual bread for his dinner guests. I think it did the trick!

Grape and Golden Raisin Bread

scant 4 cups white bread flour, plus extra for dusting

1½ teaspoons salt

2 tablespoons superfine sugar

1 oz/30 g yeast, crumbled

¼ stick butter, softened

1¼ cups water

3 oz/75 g red seedless grapes

½ cup golden raisins

Makes 1 loaf

Put the flour, salt, sugar, yeast, and butter into a large bowl and mix together, then slowly add the water until all the flour has been incorporated (you might not need all of it). Tip out onto a lightly floured counter and, using your fingers and palms, knead for 5 minutes. Put the bread back in the bowl and let rest for 1 hour.

Line a baking sheet. Add the grapes and golden raisins to the dough and mix in well. Shape into a ball, then flatten slightly using your hand and dust the top with flour. Put onto the baking sheet and let rise for 1 hour.

Preheat the oven to 400°F/200°C. Cut a square in the top of the dough and bake for 25 minutes. Transfer to a wire rack to cool.

John Woods, the Executive Chef at the Cliveden hotel, asked me to make a bread to complement his new cheeseboard, so after various experiments I came up with this one. Its sweet, slightly nutty flavor is delicious with Stilton and the stronger French cheeses—try it as an appetizer topped with baked Camembert and cranberries.

Date, Prune, and Pecan Bread *Illustrated*

½ oz/15 g package yeast

generous 3 cups whole-wheat flour, plus extra for dusting

2 teaspoons salt

½ stick butter, softened

water to mix

¾ cup chopped pecans

scant 1 cup dates, chopped

scant ¼ cup soft, no-soak dried prunes, chopped

Makes 2 x 1lb/ 450 g loaves

Dilute the yeast in a little warm water, then put with the flour, salt, and butter into a bowl and mix well. Slowly add enough water, mixing all the time, until the dough becomes elastic. Tip out onto a lightly floured counter and knead the dough for 5 minutes. Put the dough back in the bowl and let rest for 2 hours.

Divide the dough into two pieces and incorporate half the pecans, dates, and prunes into each piece, pressing in firmly. Knead for an additional 5 minutes, then rest the loaves for 1 hour.

Preheat the oven to 400°F/200°C. Grease two 1 lb/450 g loaf pans. Flatten each loaf and roll into a sausage shape. Place the seam underneath, then taper each end. Put each loaf into a pan, seam-side down, then dust with flour and, using a knife, cut a zigzag pattern on the top. Bake for 25–30 minutes, then turn out onto a wire rack to cool.

This bread is a must on any cheeseboard. I would suggest serving it with a ripe Stilton or, failing that, try it with the creamy Savoyard cheese Reblochon—oh, and a glass of red wine.

Walnut Bread

generous 2 cups whole-wheat flour

1 cup white bread flour, plus extra for dusting

1½ teaspoons salt

1 oz/30 g yeast

scant ½ stick butter, softened

¼ cup walnut oil

1¼ cups water

1¼ cups walnut pieces

Makes 1 loaf

Put all the ingredients except the walnuts into a large bowl, then mix well with your hands for 4 minutes. When all the flour has been incorporated, tip the dough out onto a lightly floured counter and, using your fingers and the heel of your palm, knead for 5 minutes. Put the dough back in the bowl and let rise for 1 hour.

Line a baking sheet. Incorporate the walnuts into the dough, then shape into a ball and dust with white flour. Place on the baking sheet and let rise for 1 hour.

Preheat the oven to 425°F/220°C. Using a sharp knife, cut a cross into the top of the dough, then bake the bread for 30 minutes until golden. Transfer to a wire rack to cool.

This bread was originally made while I was head baker at the Dorchester Hotel in London. It was baked for the breakfast menu, but quickly made its way to the cheese trolley—it's great with most cheeses.

Walnut and Golden Raisin Bread

scant 2½ cups whole-wheat flour

⅔ cup white bread flour, plus extra for dusting

1 tablespoon salt

1 oz/30 g yeast

generous ½ stick butter, softened

1¼ cups water

1 cup walnut pieces

⅔ cup golden raisins

Makes 1 loaf

Put all the ingredients except the water, walnuts, and golden raisins into a bowl, then slowly add the water and, using your hands, bind the ingredients together. When all the flour has been incorporated, tip the dough out onto a lightly floured counter and, using your fingers and the heel of your palm, knead for 5 minutes. Put the dough back in the bowl and let rise for 2 hours.

Line a baking sheet. Incorporate the walnuts and golden raisins into the dough, then shape into a ball and make a hole in the middle with your finger. Slowly begin to open the hole until it is about 2 inches/5 cm across. Dust with white flour, then place on the baking sheet and let rise for 1 hour.

Preheat the oven to 450°F/230°C. Bake the bread for 30 minutes, or until golden, then transfer to a wire rack to cool. Serve with cheese, or at breakfast toasted, with butter.

This is a very German way of making rye bread and the apricot adds a lovely fruity kick to an already fantastic loaf. You need to start this the day before.

Apricot Rye

2 cups rye flour, plus extra for dusting

1⅓ cups white bread flour, plus extra for dusting

1 oz/30 g yeast

1½ cups water

1½ teaspoons salt

generous ½ stick butter, softened

⅓ cup dried apricots, chopped

Makes 1 loaf

Put half the rye flour, half the white flour, and all the yeast into a bowl. Then add about ¾ cup of water and mix well until you have a thick paste. Let this stand overnight for 10–12 hours.

Add the rest of the flours and water, the salt, butter, and apricots to the dough and mix well for 3 minutes, then tip out onto a lightly floured counter and knead well for 3 minutes. Put the dough back in the bowl and let rise for 1 hour.

Line a baking sheet. Shape the dough into a sausage and taper the ends. Place on the baking sheet and let rise for 1 hour.

Preheat the oven to 450°F/230°C. Rub rye flour all over the top of the dough and, using a knife, cut zigzags down the center of the loaf. Bake in the oven for 30 minutes, then transfer to a wire rack to cool.

An incredibly luxurious bread that will be eaten in one sitting. IF there is any left, use it to make extra-rich bread and butter pudding. This is definitely not a bread to count calories with!

Chocolate and Sour Cherry Bread

scant 4 cups white bread flour, plus extra for dusting

2 teaspoons salt

2 tablespoons olive oil

½ oz/15 g yeast

warm water to mix

6 oz/175 g canned black cherries, drained

7 oz/200 g package chocolate chips

Makes 2 loaves

Put the flour into a bowl with the salt, olive oil, and yeast. Slowly add the warm water and mix by hand until the dough is pliable.

Tip the dough out onto a lightly floured counter and knead for 4–7 minutes. Put the dough back in the bowl and let rest for 1 hour.

Line a baking sheet. Divide the dough into two pieces and add half the cherries to each one. (You may need to add a little more flour if the mix becomes too sloppy.) Now add half the chocolate chips to each dough. Mix well, adding a little flour if the dough becomes too soft. Shape the dough into 2 balls and flatten to about 2 inches/5 cm high. Dust heavily with flour and score diagonal lines across the top to form diamond shapes. Place on the baking sheet and let the dough rest for 1 hour.

Preheat the oven to 400°F/200°C. Bake the bread for 20–25 minutes, then transfer to a wire rack to cool.

This is comfort food at its best—rich and filling. Eat it toasted for a snack, dripping with butter or, better still, piled high with baked apples or peaches with a dollop of fresh vanilla ice cream on top.

Banana and Muesli Bread

generous 3 cups whole-wheat flour

2 teaspoons salt

½ oz/15 g yeast

½ stick butter, softened

generous 1¼ cups water

2 large bananas, chopped

1 bowl of muesli

Makes 2 loaves

Put the flour, salt, yeast, and butter into a bowl. Slowly add water to the bowl and mix carefully by hand until the dough becomes elastic. Knead the dough for 5 minutes, then cover the bowl and set aside to rest for 2 hours.

Divide the dough into two, then add a chopped banana to each, using your hands to "mash" the banana into the mixture. Your dough will now be sticky, so add enough muesli to each to regain the original texture.

Line a baking sheet. Roll each dough into a ball, then press into the bowl of muesli, so that the dough becomes completely coated. Place the loaves on the baking sheet and let rise for 1–2 hours.

Preheat the oven to 400°F/200°C. Using a knife, deeply score the top of each ball into 8 sections. Bake the loaves for 25–30 minutes, then transfer to a wire rack to cool.

I was inspired to make this bread when I visited a small artisan bakery in Tours (Loire), France. The baker produced a bread with oranges, saffron, and honey made from a traditional recipe favored by famous local poet François Rabelais. My twist was to try it with oranges and lemons—I think it works well.

Lemon and Orange Bread

2⅔ cups white bread flour, plus extra for dusting

scant ⅓ cup rye flour

1 tablespoon salt

generous ½ stick butter, softened

generous ¼ cup superfine sugar

1 oz/30 g yeast

1¼ cups water

zest of 5 lemons

zest of 6 oranges

Makes 2 small loaves or 1 large loaf

Put the flours, salt, butter, sugar, yeast, and water into a bowl and massage the dough together with your hands for 3 minutes. Tip the dough out onto a lightly floured counter, then add the zests and work them well into the dough: the dough will discolor slightly, but don't worry. Put the dough back in the bowl and let rise for 1 hour.

Line a baking sheet. If making two loaves, divide the dough into two equal pieces. Shape the dough(s) into a ball shape and push your finger down through the middle until you can feel the table underneath. Then, using a sharp knife, cut them across the top several times. Place on the baking sheet and let rise for 1 hour.

Preheat the oven to 425°F/220°C. Bake for 25 minutes, or until golden brown, then transfer to a wire rack to cool.

Toasted with butter—perfect.

Orange, Lemon, and Cherry Bread

scant 4 cups white bread flour, plus extra for dusting

1 tablespoon salt

2 tablespoons superfine sugar

scant ½ stick butter, softened

1 oz/30 g yeast

zest of 1 lemon

zest of 3 oranges

1¼ cups water

3 oz/75 g sour cherries

Makes 1 loaf

Put all the ingredients except the cherries into a bowl and mix to a dough. Tip the dough out onto a lightly floured counter and knead for 5 minutes, then put the dough back into the bowl and let rest for 1 hour.

Line a baking sheet. Add the cherries to the dough and mix well, then divide the dough into two pieces and roll each out to about 12 inches/30.5 cm long. Twist the two pieces together and place on the baking sheet, then let rise for 1 hour.

Preheat the oven to 400°F/200°C. Bake the bread for 25 minutes, then transfer to a wire rack to cool.

The subtle flavors and smells in this bread are unique. Saffron works well with dough, but you could also try mango chutney—just replace the saffron with 3 oz/75 g of the chutney: yummy!

Honey and Saffron Loaf

1⅔ cups white bread flour

1½ cups whole-wheat flour

1 oz/30 g yeast

1¼ cups water

1 tablespoon salt

⅓ cup honey

2 small boxes saffron, diluted in a little water

Makes 1 loaf

Put half the white flour, half the whole-wheat flour, and all the yeast into a bowl and add ⅔ cup of water. Whisk together and mix for 5 minutes, then let stand for 4 hours.

Add the remaining flours and water, the salt, honey, and saffron to the dough and knead well for 5 minutes. Let stand in the bowl to rest for 30 minutes.

Line a baking sheet. Shape the dough into a ball, then place on the sheet and let rise for 1 hour.

Preheat the oven to 425°F/220°C. Score around the middle of the loaf with a knife and bake for 30 minutes. Transfer to a wire rack to cool.

This bread is always a great favorite with the kids at teatime, loaded with honey or chocolate spread. For a change, serve it with cream cheese and celery as an energy-giving sandwich.

Peanut Bread

scant 4 cups white bread flour

1½ teaspoons salt

½ oz/15 g yeast

warm water to mix

¾ jar (about 2 cups) crunchy peanut butter

3½ oz/100 g caramelized peanut chips, to mix

Makes 2 loaves

Put the flour, salt, and yeast into a bowl. Slowly add warm water and mix by hand until the dough is pliable. Let stand in the bowl to rest for 1 hour.

Add the peanut butter to the dough and mix it in thoroughly. The dough will now be sticky, so begin to add the peanut chips until the dough tightens up again. Divide the dough into two pieces and let rest for 1 hour.

Grease a baking sheet. Punch any air out of the dough pieces and mold into two sausage shapes, approx. 12 inches/30.5 cm long and tapering at each end. Roll them up into a coil, then place them on the baking sheet and let prove for 1 hour.

Preheat the oven to 400°F/200°C. Using a sharp knife, score a line down the middle of each loaf and dust each lightly with flour. Bake the loaves for 20–25 minutes, then transfer to a wire rack to cool.

A bread I devised while I was in Cyprus; it's gorgeous toasted and with lashings of butter.

Almond Bread

scant 4 cups white bread flour

1 tablespoon salt

generous ¼ cup superfine sugar

scant ½ stick butter, softened

½ cup ground almonds

1 oz/30 g yeast

1¼ cups milk and water mixed

4 oz/125 g slivered almonds

Makes 1 loaf

Put the flour, salt, sugar, butter, ground almonds, and yeast into a bowl. Add the milk and water mix and blend for 2 minutes. Tip out of the bowl onto a lightly floured counter and knead with your hands until the dough becomes soft and pliable. This should take no more than 5 minutes. Put the dough back in the bowl and let rise for 1 hour.

Line a baking sheet. Tip the dough out onto your floured counter and mix in half the slivered almonds. Flatten the dough into an oval shape and cover the outside of the dough with the remaining slivered almonds. Place the dough on the baking sheet and let rise for 1 hour.

Preheat the oven to 425°F/220°C. Bake the bread for 20–25 minutes, then transfer to a wire rack to cool.

My wife's favorite Danish. Remember Valentine's Day—get baking. Probably you won't use all the pastries at once, so you can freeze the finished dough for up to 3 months. You need to start this the day before.

Apple and Golden Raisin Danish Pastries

For the pastry

1 package yeast

generous 4 cups white bread flour, plus extra for dusting

1½ teaspoons salt

generous ⅛ cup superfine sugar

water to mix

4½ sticks butter, chilled

For the filling

10 apples, peeled and cored

½ cup golden raisins

2 teaspoons ground cinnamon

2 eggs, beaten, for eggwash

apricot jelly, warmed, to glaze

For the water frosting

lemon zest, confectioners' sugar, and water

Makes about 30 Danish pastries

Dilute the yeast in a little warm water and put with the flour, salt, and sugar into a large mixing bowl. Using a wooden spoon, slowly mix in a little water until the dough becomes pliable. Tip the dough out onto a lightly floured counter and knead well until it feels elastic. Put the dough back in the bowl and let stand in the refrigerator for 1 hour.

Return the chilled dough to your floured counter and roll it into a rectangle 24 x12 inches/ 60 x 30.5 cm. Flatten the chilled butter into a rectangle about ½ inch/1 cm thick and lay it over two-thirds of the dough. Bring the uncovered third of the dough into the center, then fold the covered top third down, so that your dough is now in three layers. Return the dough to the refrigerator to chill for 1 hour.

Scatter some more flour over your counter and roll out the dough to the same-size rectangle as before. Repeat the folding process, one side on top of the other, and place the dough back in the refrigerator for 1 hour. You will need to repeat this process twice more before letting the dough rest, wrapped in plastic wrap, overnight.

Line a baking sheet. Roll out the dough to about ¼ inch/5 mm thick, then cut 5 inch/12.5 cm squares from the dough. Fold the edges into the middle so you have a package, then place each one onto the baking sheet and let rise for 2 hours at an ambient temperature (20°C+).

Meanwhile, cook the apples in a pan with a little water to soften them for 7 minutes, then add the golden raisins and cinnamon and let cool.

Spoon at least 2 tablespoons of the apple mixture into the middle of each dough square. Preheat the oven to 400°F/200°C. Brush the eggwash onto the exposed parts of the dough, and bake for 20 minutes. Take out of the oven and brush with warmed apricot jelly. Cool, then top with water frosting (see page 124).

Once you've prepared the dough and cut out the shapes, you can freeze them for use later, if you wish.

Strawberry Danish

1 quantity Danish Pastry dough (see page 121)

For the filling

140 z/400 g strawberries, cut into fourths

scant 1¼ cups extra-thick strawberry yogurt

1 can thick custard (or 14 oz/400 g fresh custard)

1 egg, beaten, for eggwash

1 packet slivered almonds

2 dessertspoons apricot jelly

Makes 30–40 Danish pastries

Make the pastry as on page 121, up to the point where it is chilled overnight. Roll out to ⅛ inch/3 mm thick and cut into 12 inch/30.5 cm long by 5 inch/12.5 cm wide pieces. If you find that you don't have enough for these lengths, don't worry; just make the lengths 6–8 inches/15–20.5 cm long.

Line several baking sheets. Add the strawberries to the yogurt and fold in the custard. Spoon some of this mixture down the middle of each of the long rectangles and fold in half lengthwise. Using a knife, cut lines into the dough widthwise about 4 inches/10 cm apart all the way along. Brush with the eggwash and sprinkle the slivered almonds all over the tops. Put the dough on the baking sheets and let rise for 1 hour.

Preheat the oven to 400°F/200°C. Bake the Danish for 20 minutes, or until golden brown. Transfer to a wire rack to cool, then cut into fingers along the width.

Put the apricot jelly in a small pan with a splash of water and bring up to boil. Brush this onto the Danish pastries and serve.

This was a favorite of mine at the Cliveden hotel in the morning, eaten with a cup of tea, while sitting by the window looking at the view across the grounds.

Pain au Raisin Danish Pastries *Illustrated*

1 quantity Danish Pastry dough (see page 121)

For the filling

3½ oz/100 g fresh custard

1½ cups raisins or golden raisins

1½ teaspoons cinnamon

1 egg, beaten, for eggwash

scant ⅓ cup apricot jelly

For the water frosting

lemon zest, confectioners' sugar, and water

Makes 40–50 Danish pastries

Make the pastry as on page 121, up to the point where it is chilled overnight.

Using a rolling pin, flatten the dough into a rectangle ⅛ inch/3 mm thick. Spread the custard over the top and sprinkle liberally with raisins or golden raisins, then add a sprinkle of cinnamon and roll the dough up into a sausage. Line several baking sheets. Cut the sausage into 1 inch/2.5 cm pieces, place flat-side down on the baking sheets and let rise for 1½ hours.

Preheat the oven to 400°F/200°C. Brush the Danish lightly with the eggwash and bake for 10–15 minutes, or until golden brown. Transfer to a wire rack and brush with warm apricot jelly. Let cool, then top with water frosting (see page 124).

This bread reminds me of a little bakery near to where I was brought up in Merseyside. On my way back from school, I would buy a Sally Lunn and eat it with butter when I got home.

Sally Lunns

2⅔ cups white bread flour, plus extra for dusting

1½ teaspoons salt

scant ¼ cup superfine sugar

scant ½ stick butter, softened

1 oz/30 g yeast

½ cup milk

½ cup water, plus extra for frosting

⅓ cup golden raisins

scant ⅓ cup candied cherries

1 teaspoon ground cinnamon

zest of 3 oranges

¾ cup confectioners' sugar

Makes 1 loaf

Put the flour, salt, sugar, butter, yeast, milk, and water into a bowl and mix together with your hands. When all the flour has been incorporated, tip the dough out onto a lightly floured counter and knead until smooth and pliable. Put the dough back in the bowl and let stand for 1 hour to rest.

Line a baking sheet. Add the golden raisins, cherries, cinnamon, and orange zest to the dough and, using an electric mixer (blade attachment) or your hands, work it in well. Shape the dough into a sausage shape by flattening out the dough and rolling it up. Place the dough on the baking sheet and let rise for 1 hour.

Preheat the oven to 400°F/200°C. Bake the dough for 20 minutes, then transfer to a wire rack to cool.

While it is cooling, make a water frosting. Tip the confectioners' sugar into a bowl, then add a little water and mix in well. Gradually add more water until the frosting coats the back of a spoon. Drizzle the frosting over the top of the bread. Cut into slices and eat with butter.

These are great toasted, with butter.

Teacakes

2⅔ cups white bread flour, plus extra for dusting

1½ teaspoons salt

scant ½ cup superfine sugar

1 teaspoon ground cinnamon

½ stick butter, softened

1 oz/30 g yeast

generous ¾ cup water

½ cup golden raisins

generous ⅓ cup candied peel

1 egg, beaten, for eggwash

Makes 10–15

Put the flour, salt, sugar, cinnamon, butter, yeast, and water into a large bowl and mix together for 2 minutes. Tip the dough out onto a lightly floured counter and knead for 5 minutes, then put back into the bowl and leave for 1 hour to rest.

Line a baking sheet. Add the golden raisins and candied peel to the dough and divide the dough into 3 oz/75 g pieces. Shape each piece into a ball and, using a rolling pin, flatten them out to 1 inch/2.5 cm thick. Place the teacakes on the baking sheet and let rise for 1 hour.

Preheat the oven to 375°F/190°C. Brush the teacakes with eggwash and bake for 15 minutes.

I wanted to go back to the way we used to make Hot Cross Buns, using real fruit rather than all dried. The result is this juicy bun—the kids will love it, and adults will too!

Hollywood Hot Cross Buns

scant 4 cups white bread flour, plus extra for dusting

1½ teaspoons salt

generous ⅓ cup superfine sugar

2 oz/50 g yeast

1¼ cups milk and water mixed

2½ oz/60 g mandarin orange segments, chopped

2½ oz/60 g peach slices, chopped

2½ oz/60 g apple slices, chopped

2 teaspoons ground cinnamon

scant ¼ cup apricot jelly, warmed, to glaze

For the crosses

generous ¾ cup water

1⅓ cups flour

2 medium eggs

Makes 15–20

Put the flour, salt, sugar, and yeast into a bowl. Slowly add enough of the milk and water mix to achieve a pliable dough. Tip out onto a lightly floured counter and knead well for 5 minutes, then put the dough back in the bowl and let rise for 1 hour.

Incorporate the mandarin oranges, peaches, apples, and cinnamon into the dough and let rise for 1 hour.

Line a baking sheet. Divide the dough into 3 oz/75 g pieces and roll each into a ball. Put them on the baking sheet and let rest for 1 hour.

Preheat the oven to 400°F/200°C. To make the crosses, whisk together the water, flour, and eggs to a smooth paste and pipe a cross on top of each bun. Bake the buns for 25 minutes, or until golden brown. Take out of the oven and brush them with warmed apricot jelly. Serve immediately.

An obvious treat for my son Joshua, and a favorite of mine when I'm watching a video on those cold winter days.

Doughnuts

1⅓ cup white bread flour, plus extra for dusting

pinch of salt

scant ½ cup superfine sugar

½ stick butter, softened

⅓ cup water

1 package yeast

vegetable or corn oil for frying

superfine sugar, to coat

Makes 5–10

Put all the ingredients except the oil and coating sugar into a large bowl and mix together, then tip out onto a lightly floured counter and knead for 5 minutes. Put the dough back in the bowl and let double in size.

Divide the dough into 3 oz/75 g pieces and shape into balls. Put on your floured counter and let rise until doubled in size.

Pour some vegetable or corn oil into a large heavy-bottom pan and heat to 325°F/170°C, or medium heat. Lower each of the doughnuts into the oil and fry until brown, then roll them over and cook the other side. (If you have a problem with rolling the doughnuts over, pierce them slightly with a knife.) The frying should take no more than 5 minutes for both sides. When they are browned, tip them straight into a bowl full of superfine sugar and coat well. Cool them on a wire rack, then enjoy with a nice cup of tea.

Sweet Treats

This has to be the easiest ice cream to make and it is absolutely delicious. Serve it stuffed into baked pears or peaches or as a sweet pancake filling—unbelievable!

Brown Bread Ice Cream

1½ cups brown bread crumbs (from Guinness and Molasses Bread, page 28)

scant ⅓ cup brown sugar

3 large eggs, separated

1 tablespoon dark rum

generous 1 cup heavy cream

¾ cup confectioners' sugar

Serves 4–6

Mix the bread crumbs and brown sugar together, then place on a baking sheet and broil for 8 minutes, or until dark and caramelized. When the mixture is cool, break up into small, bite-size pieces.

Whisk the egg whites until stiff. In a separate bowl, mix the egg yolks with the rum, then fold this mixture into the egg whites. Finally, whisk the cream and confectioners' sugar together, then, using a metal spoon, fold the cream and bread crumbs into the egg mixture. Pour into a metal container and freeze for about 4 hours before serving.

This has the edge over traditional bread and butter pudding—the buttery croissants and tartness of the blueberries really lifts this dish.

Croissant Pudding

12 butter croissants (see page 48)

½ cup blackberries, plus a few extra to serve

½ cup blueberries, plus a few extra to serve

½ cup raspberries, plus a few extra to serve

splash of kirsch

confectioners' sugar

For the sauce Anglaise

1¾ cups milk

2 vanilla beans

3 medium eggs

scant ½ cup superfine sugar

Serves 6

Preheat the oven to 350°F/180°C. Cut the croissants lengthwise and place in a large casserole dish. Sprinkle over the berries and add a splash of kirsch.

To make the sauce Anglaise, put the milk and vanilla beans in a pan and bring to a boil. Whisk the eggs and sugar together to a froth, then pour the milk onto the eggs and return to the pan. Boil for 6 minutes to reduce, then pour over the croissants in the casserole dish.

Bake in the oven for 30 minutes. Take out of the oven, then sprinkle with confectioners' sugar and caramelize with a blow torch or under the broiler. Serve with light cream and more berries.

I made this recipe for Easter some years back. It appeals to both children and adults alike.

Savarin with Chocolate Sauce and Eggs

For the savarin

3 cups white bread flour

¾ cup milk

2 oz/50 g yeast

pinch of salt

scant ⅓ cup superfine sugar

4 medium eggs

1¾ sticks butter

For the sauce

5 oz/150 g light chocolate, melted

1 carton thick custard

To decorate

apricot jelly, warmed, or warm stock syrup (½ sugar to ½ water)

mini chocolate eggs

Serves 8

To make the savarin, put all the ingredients into a bowl and mix together. Beat well for 6 minutes, or until smooth, then place in a savarin ring and let rise for 1 hour until light to touch.

Preheat the oven to 400°F/200°C. Bake the savarin for 25 minutes, or until golden brown.

Meanwhile, make the chocolate sauce by stirring the melted chocolate into the custard.

Tip the savarin out of the ring and brush with the warm apricot jelly or stock syrup, if using. Fill the center with chocolate sauce and top with mini eggs.

These muffins are great eaten warm and covered with light cream, or serve them cold as a snack. Either way, they're a winner.

Blueberry Muffins *Illustrated*

2¼ sticks butter, softened

scant 1 cup superfine sugar

4 medium eggs

1⅓ cups white bread flour

1½ teaspoons baking powder

16 paper muffin liners

2 punnets blueberries

confectioners' sugar, for dusting

Makes 16 muffins

Preheat the oven to 400°F/200°C. Cream the butter and sugar until white and fluffy, then add the eggs and mix for an additional 5 minutes. Sift in the flour and baking powder and mix into a smooth paste.

Line your muffin tray with the paper liners and drop a spoonful of the mixture into each case. Gently press the blueberries into the center of each muffin.

Bake for 12 minutes, or until a muffin springs back when pressed. Transfer to a wire rack to cool, then dust lightly with confectioners' sugar.

These muffins are just spectacular served at teatime with a dollop of clotted cream, preferably accompanying cucumber sandwiches and a cup of Earl Grey tea—anyone for tennis?

Wimbledon Muffins

2¼ sticks butter, softened

scant 1 cup superfine sugar

5 medium eggs

1⅓ cups white bread flour

1½ teaspoons baking powder

16 paper muffin liners

16 medium-size strawberries, each sliced into 3

confectioners' sugar, for dusting

Makes 16 muffins

Preheat the oven to 400°F/200°C. Cream the butter and sugar until white and fluffy, then add the eggs and mix for an additional 5 minutes. Sift in the flour and baking powder and mix into a smooth paste.

Line your muffin tray with the paper liners and drop a spoonful of the mixture into each one. Gently press the sliced strawberries into the center of each muffin.

Bake for 12 minutes, or until a muffin springs back when pressed. Transfer to a wire rack to cool, then dust lightly with confectioners' sugar.

I've included crêpes in this book mainly because they contain flour and when I was working in hotels these recipes, along with some tarts and pies, were still under the jurisdiction of the baker rather than the pastry chef.

This recipe is very simple to make and the crêpes are delicious served on a bed of cream with raspberry sauce rippled through it.

Crêpes with Bananas and Cream

1⅓ cups all-purpose flour

2 tablespoons superfine sugar

1 egg

generous ¾ cup milk

¼ cup corn oil

scant ¼ stick butter

2 bananas, chopped

1 tablespoon dark rum

generous ¾ cup whipped cream

Serves 2

Whisk together the flour, 1 heaped tablespoon of the sugar, the egg, and milk for 5 minutes. You should now have a batter mixture. Test it by dipping a spoon in and seeing if it coats the back of the spoon evenly.

Heat a little corn oil in a skillet and let smoke, then pour half a cup of the batter in the middle of the skillet. Tilt the pan to move the batter to the edges and replace on the heat for 3 minutes. Turn the crêpe over with a spatula and cook for an additional 2 minutes. Remove from the pan and put on a plate to cool. Repeat with the rest of the batter.

To make the filling, drop the butter into the skillet, then add the bananas and cook for 1 minute. Add the rum and flambé until the flames die down. Cook for an additional 2 minutes and let the side.

Whisk up the cream with the remaining sugar and spoon a little into the middle of each crêpe. Top with the bananas, then roll up and serve on a pool of light cream, if so desired—watch those waistlines!

My father and mother were both excellent at making pastry and I grew up knowing how to make good sweet pastry. Some pastry work is essential to becoming a good baker—it gives you a little edge on the competition.

I had this tart in Chinon in the Loire with a glass of Chablis for lunch—delicious!

Normandy Apple Tart

For the paste

2½ cups white bread flour, plus extra for dusting

1¼ cups superfine sugar

1 stick butter, softened

1 medium egg

splash of water to mix

4 dessert apples, thinly sliced

scant ¼ cup apricot jelly, warmed

For the frangipane

1¾ sticks butter, softened

1 cup superfine sugar

2 medium eggs plus 2 medium egg yolks

splash of calvados

generous ⅓ cup all-purpose flour

1⅔ cups ground almonds

Serves 8

Preheat the oven to 400°F/200°C. To make the sweet paste, put the flour, sugar, butter, egg, and water into a bowl and combine. Roll out on a lightly floured counter and use to line a 12 inch/30.5 cm shallow round cake pan.

To make the frangipane, cream the butter and sugar together and add the eggs and egg yolks one at a time. Add the Calvados, flour, and ground almonds and mix well. Spread the frangipane over the paste in the cake ring, then fan out the apple slices from the edge to the middle in the form of a cross.

Bake for 25 minutes, or until golden brown. Brush with apricot jelly while still warm and serve immediately.

My twist on the traditional English recipe. The addition of real fruit lifts the pies to new heights. Remember when lining the tins to keep the pastry thin and add plenty of filling.

Hollywood Mince Pies

For the pastry

2½ cups white bread flour

2¼ sticks butter, softened

½ cup superfine sugar, plus extra for sprinkling

1 medium egg

splash of water to mix

For the filling

2 jars mincemeat

½ large can of mandarin oranges, drained and chopped

2 apples, finely diced

Makes 25 pies

Preheat the oven to 400°F/200°C. To make the sweet pastry, rub the flour, butter, sugar, and egg together with a splash of water to make a paste. If using a mixer, use the paddle and mix for 2 minutes. Do not overmix.

To make the filling, turn the mincemeat out into a bowl, then throw the mandarin oranges and apples into the bowl and blend in by hand.

Use deep muffin tins. Rip off a small piece of sweet paste and line the sides and bottom of each mold. Fill each one with a good helping of the mincemeat mixture so that it reaches three-quarters of the way up the side of the mold.

Using a rolling pin, roll out your lids and cut to slightly bigger than the top of the tins. Place a lid on top of each pie and gently push down. Prick the lids with a knife and sprinkle with sugar.

Bake for 20 minutes, then transfer to a wire rack to cool. Serve warm with fresh cream.

A very French recipe my mother-in-law is famous for. The cinnamon really adds another dimension to this pie.

Apple Pie

For the pastry

2½ cups white bread flour

1¼ cups superfine sugar

1 stick butter, softened

1 medium egg

⅔ cup ground almonds

For the filling

3 lb/1.4 kg apples, peeled, cored and sliced

splash of Calvados

juice of 3 lemons

handful of golden raisins

pinch of cinnamon

For the topping

1 egg, beaten, for eggwash

superfine sugar, for sprinkling

Serves 6

Soak the sliced apples in the Calvados and lemon juice for 2 hours. Mix all the pastry ingredients together and let rest for 1 hour.

Preheat the oven to 400°F/200°C. Roll out the pastry to fit into a 12 inch/30.5 cm pie pan or foil base and fill with the apples and golden raisins. Sprinkle with cinnamon. Roll out the pastry trimmings for the lid, then cover the pie and crimp the edges together. Brush with the eggwash and sugar and bake for 25 minutes, or until golden brown.

I was first introduced to sweet pastry by my mother Gill—she gave me this recipe and it's the best! The pastry will keep, covered in plastic wrap, in the refrigerator for 1 week.

Apple and Pear Pie with Fruit Sauce *Illustrated*

For the pastry

2½ cups white bread flour

1¼ cups superfine sugar

1 stick butter, softened

1 medium egg

2 tablespoons water

For the filling

8 apples, peeled, cored, and chopped

8 pears, peeled, cored, and chopped

scant ¼ cup sugar

For the topping

1 egg, beaten, for eggwash

superfine sugar, for sprinkling

For the sauce

2 punnets raspberries

confectioners' sugar

Serves 6

Preheat the oven to 400°F/200°C. To make the pastry, using a beater on an electric mixer, blend all the ingredients together to make a smooth pastry.

To make the filling, put the fruit and sugar into a pan and cook over medium heat for 5 minutes to soften the fruit.

Roll the pastry out onto a 12 inch/30.5 cm pie plate and spoon on the filling. Roll out the excess pastry to make the lid and place on top. Trim the pastry edges and crimp around the edge, then brush with eggwash and sprinkle with sugar. Bake for 25 minutes, or until golden brown.

Meanwhile make the raspberry sauce. Pass the raspberries through a strainer, then stir in a little confectioners' sugar. Serve with the pie.

Index